The Falmouth Packets

1689–1851

Tony Pawlyn

Truran

Published by Truran 2003

Truran is an imprint of Truran Books Ltd Croft Prince, Mount Hawke, Truro,
Cornwall TR4 8EE
www.truranbooks.co.uk

Printed and bound in Cornwall by R. Booth Ltd, Antron Hill, Mabe, Penryn,
Cornwall TR10 9HH

Acknowledgements

Working on this book has been a great pleasure, and I hope you will all enjoy my account of
the Falmouth Packet Service. It has taken a couple of years to bring this book to publication,
but it embraces elements of research going back more than 30 years. Along the way so many
friends have given me help and encouragement that it is impossible to mention them here.
Nevertheless, it would be wrong not to thank my friends and colleagues Mark Myers and
Ralph Bird. Mark for his exquisite vignettes and Ralph for his redrafting of the packet plans;
Edward Yescombe and Roger Owen, for their ready exchange of packet information and
sources; my friends at the Bartlett Library, National Maritime Museum Cornwall, and in the
South West Maritime History Society, for their support and encouragement over the years. In
no particular order I thank the National Maritime Museum, Greenwich for the use of the
stirring 'Rogers' portrait. Heritage, Royal Mail for their help with the surviving Packet Archives
(many of which have still to be searched properly). Terry Knight and his staff at the Cornwall
Studies Library, Redruth, for their ever-friendly welcome and assistance. And, to George
Hogg and the staff of the new National Maritime Museum Cornwall, for their support and
encouragement and for allowing me to commandeer all the packet books for many months..
To my publishers, Heather and Ivan Corbett, I owe a great debt of thanks, firstly for proposing
the project, and then for their constant editorial help, enthusiasm and encouragement along
the way. Though I hope there are not too many, the inevitable mistakes are all mine.

Dedication
Though she has no interest in 'boats', this book is for Val,
my chosen partner through eternity

Contents

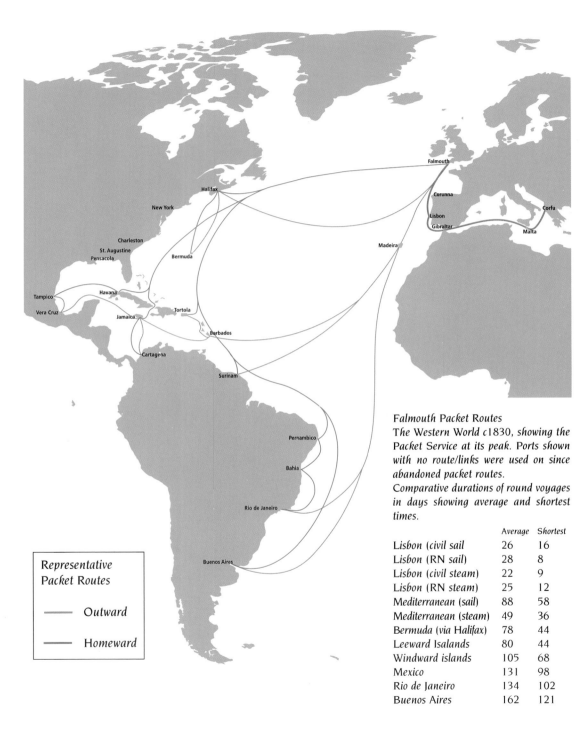

Falmouth Packet Routes
The Western World c1830, showing the
Packet Service at its peak. Ports shown
with no route/links were used on since
abandoned packet routes.
Comparative durations of round voyages
in days showing average and shortest
times.

	Average	Shortest
Lisbon (civil sail	26	16
Lisbon (RN sail)	28	8
Lisbon (civil steam)	22	9
Lisbon (RN steam)	25	12
Mediterranean (sail)	88	58
Mediterranean (steam)	49	36
Bermuda (via Halifax)	78	44
Leeward Isalands	80	44
Windward islands	105	68
Mexico	131	98
Rio de Janeiro	134	102
Buenos Aires	162	121

Representative
Packet Routes

—— Outward

—— Homeward

Introduction

In the morning of the 1st October, the man at the mast-head called out a sail; we were soon convinced that all hopes of escape, by swiftness, were vain. We therefore had the netting stuffed with hammocks and sails, the arms all prepared, and the hands at quarters.

The enemy began to fire at about 40 minutes past eleven A.M. but as his shot did not reach us, we did not return his fire till about half past twelve, and so continued till he closed, and grappled us on the starboard quarter, at about a quarter past one. In this situation it became quite calm, and the vessels could not have separated even had they been inclined. As soon as they grappled us, our boarders were prepared with their pikes, but our nettings were so lofty, and so well secured, that they did not attempt to board: our pikemen, again flew to their muskets, pistols, and blunderbusses; our Captain all the while giving his orders with admirable coolness, and encouraging his men by his speeches and example, in such a way, that there was no thought of yielding, although many heroes now lay stretched upon deck in their blood; but then we saw the enemy's deck completely covered with their dead and wounded, and the fire from our great guns doing dreadful execution at every discharge. We now began to hear them scream, which so inspired our gallant little crew, that many of the wounded returned again to their quarters. At length, about a quarter past three, the rascals ran from their quarters; when our Captain, with five or six of his brave comrades, rushed on board, killed their Captain, tore down their colours, and drove the few remaining on deck below, and the privateer surrendered. –

Our force consisted of a small ship of 180 tons, mounted with six 4-pounders and two sixes, and manned by 28 people, officers and boys included, of which there were 4 of the latter under 17 years of age. The privateer was called the Genii, is the most complete out of Guadeloupe, mounting six long sixes, and one long 18 pounder, fixed upon a swivel in the centre of her main deck, and traversing upon a circle, so that this enormous piece of ordnance was worked just as easily as a common swivel; and having on board, at the commencement of the fight 86 men, of which number 26 were killed, or died in a few hours, and 30 more were wounded. Both vessels were greatly damaged in the action, and it was not till six o'clock that we were disengaged from each other. On our side we lost three brave fellows, two of whom were killed on the spot, and the third died the same evening; another, I fear, is mortally wounded through breast and shoulder. We had besides, nine others wounded, and three or four of them badly.

Charleston Ferry Boat 1730

The above account was written by a passenger soon after his arrival at Falmouth in November 1807. Such reports proliferate the annals of British naval history and were fairly typical of small ship actions during the French Revolutionary and Napoleonic, wars. However, on this occasion the victorious vessel was no Royal Naval warship, but a civil packet carrying mails and passengers. The vessel concerned was the **Windsor Castle**, a Falmouth packet employed in the service of the

British Royal Mail, and while technically a 'Crown' ship, she was in reality a defensively armed merchant vessel. This makes her victory over a heavily armed and manned enemy privateer, even the more remarkable.

This account is just one of many emanating from this period, though not all such actions were so honourably fought, nor so successfully concluded. To the mass of the British general public, the accompanying 'butcher's bill' said it all – determining in their minds the nature of the fight and the relative merits of the participants. As a result of their bravery, Captain Rogers, the temporary commander of the **Windsor Castle**, and his valiant crew received significant rewards, as well a share of the prize money raised by the sale of the **Genii**, alias the **Le Jeune Richard** (upon which even the official accounts cannot agree).

In writing this book I have set out to give an insight into the nature of the men and vessels employed in this service. A service which ran without interruption from the late 1680s to the 1850s, through times of war and peace. These vessels – for the most part little ships and brigs – carried governmental and commercial dispatches and letters, across the length and breadth of the oceans of the Western hemisphere. The day to day service was routine and humdrum, but knowledge was power and the news and information carried were vital to the political and mercantile aspirations of the emerging British Empire.

The cost of this service was rarely covered by the mail conveyed, and in the pragmatic commercial world of merchant seamen, there were many who were incredulous at such an expensive misuse of shipping capacity. The pilot guiding the packet **Speedy** (1), up to Quebec in September 1784, was typically sceptical:

> Tho our pilot had now been on board more than three days he could not tell what to make of the ship. It was not a Man of War he could see by the Guns nor could he see any thing like Merchandise. At length his curiosity was raised to so high a pitch he could contain it no longer, and after making a great many apologys he begged to know what the ship was Loaded with. Capt. D'Auverne produced a small Mail containing about fifty Letters which he said was all his loading but the Lt Houghton had five more which was the Only Reason for sending the ship. He Laughed at this nor was it easy to make him believe this kind of loading was very common & that a great many ships were kept for no other purpose.

The normal cargo of a Falmouth packet did indeed consist of a few bundles of mail, contained in one or more heavy leather portmanteaus, but passengers, and freights of bullion and specie were also carried.

In the opening years of the 21st century very few people, familiar as they are with all the home comforts and facilities of luxury cruise liners, will have considered that the distant origins of these splendid vessels lay in the humble mail packets of the 17th and 18th centuries. Soon after its inception, the carriage of fare-paying passengers was encouraged as a means of subsidising the packet service. It was by no means cheap travel, but the mail packets offered one of the few dependable modes of transport between Great Britain and her dominions, colonies and allies located around the Atlantic rim. In times of war and peace, diplomatic and military personnel, along with their entourages, gentlemen travellers with their servants and merchants with their families, all relied heavily on the Falmouth packets to carry them to and from their home and foreign duty stations.

Later, in the mid-nineteenth century, valuable mail contracts subsidised the embryo steamship companies – the Peninsular Steam Navigation Company; the Royal Mail Line; the Cunard Line, and their like. Their steamers drove the sailing packets from the seas, opening the way for establishing great fortunes, and laying the ground for the construction of massive ocean liners and their ultimate successors the cruise liners. 'The rest', as they say 'is history'.

What remains of Samuel Trefusis' Great Cellar, built in 1709 for the use of the Post Office Packet Service, backs onto the main street through Flushing and is marked by this modern plaque

1 'Pacquets' – the Post Office Packet Service at Falmouth

Packet Brigantine 1740

The Post Office Packet Service was a branch of the British Royal Mail, established to carry the international mails to and from Great Britain. State letters and dispatches were known by the generic term of 'pacquets' or packets, after the French *paquet* – which alluded to the way in which the dispatches were packaged and sealed for carriage. In time the organisation carrying these dispatches became known as the 'pacquet service', and vessels employed in that service as pacquet boats, packet boats, or *paquebot*. One of the earliest references to these comes from a Treasury minute of 1598:

> *Postes towards Ireland, Hollyhead, allowance as well for serving the packett by lande as for entertaining a bark to carie over and return the packet, x pounds (£10) the moneth.*

During the reign of Charles I, the 'King's Post' was opened to the public for the first time in a bid to recoup some of the cost, but it took some time before the modern concept of the King's Post Office, or Royal Mail took shape.

From time immemorial, long distance overland dispatch services, had been carried by messengers working in stages between relay stations – either on foot or on horseback – where remounts and refreshments were provided. Throughout the British Isles the inland mails were now carried by relays of 'post-boys' of all ages. As the volume of post increased, and the public roads were improved, mail-carts and mail coaches were introduced. Soon after the introduction of scheduled mail coaches, the carriage of passengers was first permitted, to help subsidise the service. Many of the established way-stations then became wayside inns.

Prior to the introduction of the postage stamp and the universal (inland) 'Penny Post', the British method of charging for mail was payment on delivery – post-payment. The cost of postage was assessed by the number of charging zones a letter passed through on its journey, and could not be calculated until it reached its final delivery zone. This in turn gave rise to the generic term for mail as 'the post', and later the departmental name of the Post Office.

The British Post Office's inland routes were soon well organised and controlled, but the sea links between Britain and overseas postal authorities were less well regulated. Quite early on two mail routes were established between England and the Continent – Dover to Calais (and/or Ostend), and Harwich to Helvoetsluys – the Hook of Holland. The other long established sea link was the Irish Mail (noted in 1598), running between Dublin and Holyhead, but this was regarded as a domestic link rather than an international service. The security of our international mails was brought sharply into focus soon after the

Protestant William of Orange became King of England in 1689. Great Britain became embroiled in conflict with Roman Catholic France, and the established overland postal routes across France, via Paris to both the Iberian Peninsula, and the Mediterranean, were closed. The overland routes to central Europe and the Ottoman Empire and beyond were easily re-routed through Holland, but a major sector of our commercial links lay with Spain and Portugal, and through them with the Americas and the West Indies. Increasing commercial pressures, as well as political necessity, made the establishment of a completely new route to the Iberian Peninsula highly imperative, and the Falmouth Packet Service was conceived.

Such a move had been contemplated in 1674, by Colonel Whitley, the then Post Master General (PMG), who advised the postmaster at Plymouth, that he:

> *... may have to send the letters... to Spain and Portugal (which now go by Paris) ... by establishing 3 or 4 Pacquet Boates at Plymouth, Foy or some other Westerne Porte... which may also carry passengers, goods, etc, being Lycenced by the Customs Officers.*

This plan was not however immediately adopted, and it was some fifteen years later before the service was established. The precise date of the birth of the packet service between Falmouth and the Groyne of Corunna, is not certain, though 1688/89 has been widely quoted. It was certainly well established by the early 1690s, and as a diplomatic gesture to our Spanish allies, the first two Falmouth packets were named **Spanish Allyance**, and **Spanish Expedition**.

But why was Falmouth chosen as the English terminus for this new service? In the 1680s Falmouth was little more than a provincial village with newly acquired town status, having received its charter from Charles II on August 20th 1660. Vigorously promoted by Sir Peter Killigrew of Arwenack, and centred on the hamlet of Smithick, Sir Peter had first procured the rights and privileges of a regular market in 1652. His new town enjoyed a good supply of fresh water – essential to support any shipping trade, and an Act of Parliament, encouraged Sir Peter to build new quays, which were completed by 1670. Perhaps Sir Peter's commercial aspirations, coupled to the rapid growth of the town, led to its tongue in cheek appellation 'Pennycomequick', but the name of Falmouth was the one that stood the test of time.

Falmouth's chief drawback was its distance from London, a long way from the centres of government and commerce. And the King's Great Post Road from Cornwall to London (the Great Western Road), was little more than a hardcore track. For much of the way between Falmouth and Exeter it followed the old ridgeway, keeping to the drier high ground whenever possible. Along these sections it was reasonably passable in most seasons. But, where it inevitable descended to cross

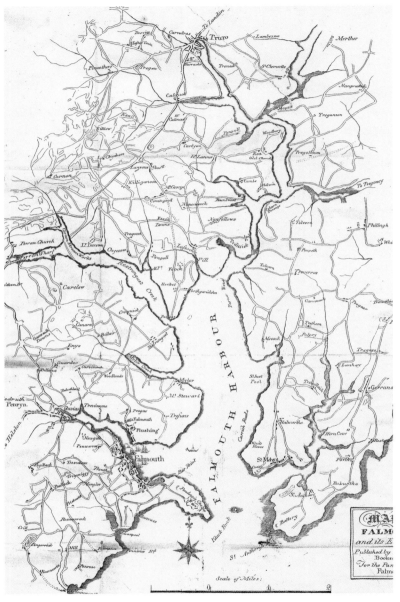

lowland sections and river valleys, there were long stretches of treacherous boggy ground, to impede the progress of even the stoutest travellers.

While the distance by road was daunting, and the condition of that road deplorable, these were not the determining factors in establishing a terminal port for the new overseas postal service. The terminal port had to be:
– sufficiently far away from the French coast to prevent seizure of the packets by privateers
– a good haven offering secure shelter from the wind and weather
– at a location sufficiently well fortified to deter raids by enemy shipping
– situated well to the westward to allow the best offing [clearance from the land] for sailing packets setting out against the prevailing westerly winds
– the shortest sea route to enable the quickest passages, and reduce the risk of total loss of the mail due to shipwreck or enemy force.

River Fal, c1820
giving a clear indication of the sheltered anchorage off Falmouth, the guarded entrance
to the estuary, and the tortuous route of the old post road to Truro
(The Cornwall Centre)

The mouth of the river Fal met all the requirements of a terminal port for the embryo mail service. It was the south-western most haven port of the British mainland. A deep estuary, it was surrounded by hilly ground, and contained good shelter and numerous anchorages. Its entrance and waters were protected by the headland fortresses of Pendennis and St. Mawes.

When first enchartered the new town of Falmouth lay within the old customs out-port of Penryn, while up river parts of the Fal estuary comprised the customs out-port of Truro. This situation was not conducive to the growth of the new town, and in 1675–76 a commission was appointed to examine rival claims and set the port limits of Falmouth. By this commission Falmouth was established as a customs out-port under Plymouth, with legal quays, a custom house, and duly appointed customs officers. When these rights and limits were challenged in 1703, a new commission (warranted on December 22nd 1703) settled the issue for once and for all. But, at the same time it established the additional customs out-port of Helford, with a custom house at Gweek. This meant that there were then four custom houses within a radius of eight miles, creating a complex bureaucratic situation not to be found anywhere else in the British Isles.

Fortunately, as *non-trading* vessels, the packets were allowed to put to sea without formal clearance at a custom house, so the initial wrangling did not effect the packet service. Once established, the Falmouth Packet Station proved invaluable to the machinery of state and ultimately to the administration of our western colonies, as well as a boon to our merchant adventurers. Despite significant financial costs, and almost constant Treasury carping, the packet service out of Falmouth proved too valuable to contemplate its loss. In time new routes were added, existing routes modified, or occasionally withdrawn. This latter course was often only a temporary expedient, and in most instances the services were re-instated at a later date. Throughout it all the Falmouth Packet Service grew and prospered, and hand in hand with it the town of Falmouth developed and expanded.

Falmouth v Flushing

While Sir Peter Killigrew had been extremely active during the late sixteen hundreds, promoting his new town and port in political and court circles, the Trefusis family had been almost as active in trying to turn their seaside hamlet of Flushing into a thriving seaport. A specific date for the founding of Flushing cannot be ascribed, but it was a recognised place by the time Killigrew obtained his Royal Charter for Falmouth in 1661. The Cornish historian Thomas Tonkin (1678–1742) recorded that the Trefusis family, had been at *no small expenses in levelling the place, building quays etc: for loading and unloading vessels.* Tradition has it that Dutch workmen executed this work, and possibly bestowed upon it the port name from their homeland. Tonkin's chronology may be a little suspect, but it is probable that the original quay works were started well before the Civil War.

Samuel Trefusis (1676–1724) added extensively to these works. A reservoir had been created in the Nankersey valley, with conduits

Flushing Waterfront Little docks and quays such as these formed a key part of the infrastructure of Flushing and Little Falmouth. While the packets were normally kept afloat, facilities such as these enabled them to be laid up when required for overhaul and essential repairs

leading down to a holding tank behind the quay at Flushing. This connected with a large spigot outlet on the quay, the use of which was controlled by securing it behind a heavy locked door. Samuel was only twelve or thirteen years old when the Post Office packets were first stationed at Falmouth, and the packets needed from five to ten thousand gallons of fresh water for long voyages. As he grew towards his majority he determined to draw key elements of the packet service to his village, seeing it as a major factor in improving the fortunes of the Trefusis estate. In particular he focused on the victualling of the packets, packet servicing and the provision of storage facilities and a range of housing accommodation.

His objectives were clear; in 1702 at the age of 26 Samuel Trefusis married Alice Cotton, one of Sir Robert Cotton's daughters – Sir Robert then being one of the concurrent PMG (1691–1708). In 1719, shortly after Alice's death, Samuel married Margaret Craggs, the daughter of another PMG, in St. Paul's Cathedral – just to ensure his continuity of interest and influence. With one or other PMG sympathetic to Samuel's well-being, Flushing's future seemed assured,and Samuel obtained a ruling that all commanders, officers, and seamen *must live in Flushing, or forfeit their jobs*. This rule did not stay

The Great Cellars These units are all that remains of the warehouse at Flushing, built by Samuel Trefusis in 1709. The arched cellars give a clear indication of their original substantial construction

in force for very long, but by the time it lapsed many had already established their roots in Flushing, and it was a pleasant place to live. Zachary Rogers, the third agent of packets at Falmouth (1705–13), is known to have been stationed there, as may have been Durdin (1713–15) and Penhallow (1715–23).

Samuel set about building warehouses as well as basic housing for seamen in the lower part of the village, together with more substantial housing for the packet commanders and their families, a little further up the hill. In 1709 he made a good deal with the Post Office, when they paid him £611 17s 4d for the use of the warehouse, together with an annual rent. However there was some dispute when the warehouse turned out much bigger than anticipated. This extra space was rented out to individual packet commanders for storing surplus gear and reserve items of ship's equipment. It was a substantial building. The ground floor consisted of stone built, vaulted cellars, with a run of lofts above, and a further two floors of timber built accommodation above that again. The two upper floors disappeared years ago, and only a small part of the original building now remains.

Just how long the packet agency remained at Flushing is not certain. From a postal point of view Flushing was a little off the beaten track and by 1724 agent Stephen Banfield was living in Falmouth. Even so, with a reliable supply of fresh water, ample storage buildings, a range of good housing, and a pleasant southerly location, Flushing remained a strategic spot for servicing the packets for many generations. In addition a number of later packets were built at Little Falmouth, just half a mile further up the Penryn river, and conveniently close to the packet commanders' homes.

Falmouth to London by Road

Falmouth's distance from London (273 miles), and the attendant problems of carrying the mail and bullion to and fro, were a constant niggle. However, prior to the mid-nineteenth century, this was never sufficiently seriously a drawback as to threaten Falmouth's status as a packet station.

The almost feudal arrangements for maintaining the King's Post Road, whereby each parish was responsible for maintaining its section of the road, did little to improve it from a rural cart track. It was not until the formation of the new turnpike trusts that any significant improvements were made, and then not until the middle years of the eighteenth century. Even then improvements were piecemeal. Different turnpike trusts were responsible for different lengths of the road, with many unregulated intermediate sections. However, despite the condition of the road, by strategic staging, the journey time for the conveyance of the mails was brought down to three to four days by the mid-eighteenth century. Other improvements followed.

While the regular mail coach through Exeter to Falmouth may not have been established until 1798, there were a number of earlier attempts at establishing regular passenger coach services between

New Quay Lodge, New Quay House, and Rockside
These elegant but functional Georgian houses on the Flushing waterfront were once the homes of packet commanders

without expence in alterations, having lately been papered and fitted
up with neat marble chimney pieces, locks, bolts, bells, &c.
   Enquire on the premises; or of William Spicer, Esq; of Wear,
near Exeter.—Dated July 22, 1776.

This is to acquaint the Nobility, Gentry, Merchants,
and Others, That

The Old Exeter Stage-Coach,

On Steel Springs, for the better accommodation of Passengers, is removed from the New Inn, in Fore-street, Exeter, lately kept by Mr.
Thomas Parker, to the house of Mr. John Hemmings, known by the
sign of the Half Moon, next the said New Inn.
   Likewise, The PLYMOUTH STAGE COACH, on Steel Springs,
is removed from the London Inn, in Plymouth, to Mr. John Keenor's,
at the Bristol Inn, late the White Hart Inn, in Old Town, Plymouth,
near the Shambles.
   Each inside passenger to pay from Plymouth to Exeter 10s. 6d.
From Plymouth to London, 2l. 2s.   Outside passengers as usual.
   Likewise, on Tuesday the 13th of August set out from the said
Half-Moon Inn, in Fore-street, Exeter, A POST DILIGENCE, in
Thirty Hours, to London, except in case of accidents, and will continue every Tuesday, Thursday, and Saturday mornings, at Six o'clock,
to the Bell Inn, in Friday-street, London; and will set out at the same
time, each day, from the said Bell Inn, in Friday-street, London, for
Exeter, to be down in the same time, carrying Three Inside Passen-
gers, at Three-pence per mile.
   The favours already received, and the continuance of them, will always be gratefully acknowledged, by   Their humble servants,
            ILIFFS, PARTRIDGE, BIRD, and Co.
   ☞ The Bath Machine sets off from the said Half Moon Inn every
Monday and Friday mornings.

To be LETT, and entered upon at Lady-Day next, for
a term of seven years,

ALL those Five CLOSES of LAND,
   consisting of thirty and three acres of arable, meadow, and
pasture ground, with the appurtenances, known by the name of

Falmouth and Exeter. Some mail may have been carried by these
as it is extremely doubtful if relays of post-boys could have
managed the high volume of overseas mails that were passing
between London, Exeter and Falmouth by the 1780s. If not mail
coaches, then at least closed mail carts must have been
introduced many years earlier to cope with the growing
requirements of the service.

By the late eighteenth century journey times had been further
reduced, and in 1798 the packets of mail made up in London on a
Wednesday, were expected to be delivered at Falmouth, and
shipped on board a packet, ready to sail on the Saturday – near
enough two and a half days, which remained the norm of many
decades.

As far as packet passengers travelling between London
and Falmouth were concerned, the overland journey was never to
attain a much higher standard. It got a little quicker, but not by
much. And it was not without its hazards:

> On Friday night, as the mail-coach was passing over Poulson Bridge,
> which separates Cornwall from Devonshire, one of the wheels came in

contact with an angle in the wall, and the coach overset. There were four outside passengers on the coach; three of whom were precipitated over the bridge; the fourth hung by his hands on the top of the wall, until he was delivered by the guard. A Mr. Williams of London, one of the passengers, had his right leg badly fractured, and one of his ribs broken; another a Portuguese, received several wounds and contusions in different parts of his body; the third escaped with a slight wound on his knee. The coachman was seriously hurt and the guard slightly.

The West Briton August 14th 1812

The risks of the English Channel were often preferred to the rough riding by stagecoach, and it was also a cheaper mode of travel. Such passages, made under sail, took about a week on average, but could be accomplished in two or three days, given a fair wind. After 1825, the sea journey to and from Falmouth was greatly improved in terms of speed, regularity and comfort, by the introduction of the coastal paddle steamer **Sir Francis Drake**, and shortly after, her consort the **Brunswick**. Having proved their reliability, they attracted quite a following, regularly conveying passengers between Falmouth and Plymouth, and on to Portsmouth, in the season. The final leg from Portsmouth to London was at first conducted by fast coaches, then the *Western Steam Carriage*, and finally by railway trains. This brought the overall travelling time between Falmouth and London down to about thirty-five hours, in 1834. Some further improvement was achieved after the railway reached Plymouth in 1848, but by then the Falmouth Packet Service was in terminal decline. When the railway connection between Devon and Cornwall was finally made, it was eight years too late to save the Falmouth packets.

Falmouth Harbour c1825
*Looking south-east the old waterfront is clearly identifiable today. Amongst a host of sailing craft is the early steam packet **Sir Francis Drake**. Established on the Falmouth to Plymouth run in that year, she remained in service until 1865*
(The Cornwall Centre)

2 Post Office Packet Organisation

West Indian Sloop,
Barbados 1760

The packet service was, to all intents and purposes, just another department of the General Post Office. It fell under the corporate responsibility of the PMG – an office which, while referred to in the singular, was concurrently filled by two individuals between 1691 and 1823. The post holders usually changing with the government of the day, day to day administration of the packet service, along with other departments, was the responsibility of the secretary to the PMG, officially the Secretary of the Post Office. And, while the office of PMG was a politically sensitive one, the post of secretary was more stable, becoming a career post within the established Civil Service. Amongst the more influential secretaries were Anthony Todd, (c1762–65, and 1768–1798), and Francis Freeling (1798–1836). Freeling had been resident surveyor at Post Office headquarters for five years before being promoted to secretary. In particular he was responsible for seeing through the many reforms and improvements started by Anthony Todd. He was especially adept in persuading others to conform, while remaining firm but fair in applying new regulations. His insistence that the rules applied equally to all commanders at Falmouth did much to eliminate the abuses that had crept in over the years, and curb the cavalier attitude of a number of the older commanders.

As the administration and management of the packet service grew more onerous, additional personnel were appointed, both at headquarters and at Falmouth, to ensure the smooth running of the packet service.

Inspector of Packets

In the early 1790s the duties of an Inspector of Packets were introduced, which were undertaken by one John Burnett Bennett. Despite a number of attempts to get Bennett admitted as a member of staff, these were all rejected by the Treasury. Thus, from 1790 to 1805, Bennett appears to have been employed as an unestablished consultant – albeit with far reaching influence. From 1790 he was employed by the day, at 7s 6d per day plus 10s 6d per day travelling expenses – equivalent to a salary of £300 per annum, with additional sums for subsistence being allowed when he was on the road inspecting packets etc. Eventually in 1805 he became a member of staff on a salary of £350 p.a. considerably less than those of the six regional Riding Surveyors (£600 p.a.), to whom he considered himself equal if not superior. Up to this time he was also carried on the books of Deptford Dock Yard, as a Quarterman Shipwright – without pay.

Bennett's duties seem quite flexible. His was a roving commission, involving considerable travel all round the country.

Bennett was constantly on the move between headquarters, the different packet stations, and shipbuilding centres. Based on London, he was responsible for examining new packets in the course of construction; ascertaining damage sustained by packets in maritime accidents, or from enemy action; assessing and valuing packets for compensation purposes; and checking on the suitability of temporary packets offered for hire during periods of emergency. In addition he was often called on to advise the PMG on a whole range of packet related procedures and matters, which seems to have given him a inflated sense of importance.

Bennett was firmly convinced of his indispensability in the running of the service, but he eventually blotted his copybook during the packet mutiny of 1810. Having been instrumental in resolving the little known packet mutiny of 1801, he failed to advise his superiors of the action then taken. His uncharacteristic reticence may have resulted from trying to bring down the new agent at Falmouth – Christopher Saverland, who had previously been a Riding Surveyor based on London. Although not appreciated at the time, Bennett's reserved position was soon exposed, drawing down Francis Freeling's barely veiled ire:

> … Mr. Bennett has found it necessary in many cases to oppose Measures not originating with himself; to inveigh against the just and approved Claims of a deserving Set of Men, & to lose Sight of the Necessity of Encouragement to the due Performance of one of the most arduous and important Services of the State, and that I have felt all the Embarrassments of his peculiar and tenacious Character for some years past is in ample Evidence before your Lordships, and your Predecessors

Freeling had learnt that Bennett could have prevented the second packet mutiny, and the only surprise is that Bennett was not sacked then and there. It was about this time that Freeling's son George Henry, then about 21, was appointed to assist his father as the Assistant Secretary of the Post Office, with particular responsibility for the packet service. Though checked, Bennett survived another four years, before being pensioned off in 1814/15. He was then about 60 years of age, and just prior to this his salary had been increased to £600 p.a., possibly in order to enhance his pension.

The Packet Agents

These were the key appointees, on whom the smooth and efficient running of the Falmouth Packet Station depended. Initially local men were chosen to fill the post, and their duties were limited to the receipt and dispatch of mails to and from London, and ensuring the regular supply of stores and provisions for the packets. In so far as the day to day regulation of the packet service was concerned, full responsibility originally lay with the packet contractor – Edward Dummer. On his death in 1714, the Post Office encouraged several different contractors to tender to supply packet ships, and the management of the packets and co-ordination of the service at Falmouth fell to the packet agent. The agent's duties covered the whole range of service related activities, including:

- implementing the PMG's instructions, and reporting to and liaising with the secretary at headquarters
- ensuring that packet commanders complied with the terms of their contracts
- arranging Captains' courts to investigate any personal or operational irregularities
- approving and appointing local contractors to supply all kinds of stores, materials, and victuals, for the packet service
- regulating the regular dispatch and receipt of the mails to and from London, and supervising the arrival and sailing of the packets.

The first Agent of Packets appointed at Falmouth was one Daniel Gwyn, (Gwynn, or Gwin), with an annual salary of £70. The new packet station was so remotely situated from London, that Gwyn was virtually a law unto himself. For an unscrupulous agent the temptations were many. Within his sphere of operations lay numerous opportunities to extract commissions to enhance his basic salary. Contemporary attitudes to what in modern times would be termed graft and corruption, were lax and sympathetic. Most people in public office expected or demanded, payments over and beyond their official fees and remuneration. A man of his times, Gwyn's business morality does not appears to have been any better or worse than most of his peers. During a part, if not all of his time as Agent of Packets at Falmouth, Gwyn was also the Collector of Customs (the highest office in that service at an out-port), postmaster, and Collector of the Salt Duty (then an Excise post). Neither Gwyn, nor his employers, saw anything wrong with this, though to the modern view there were some obvious conflicts of interest, especially given the packetmen's attitude to free trade.

Gwyn was an entrepreneur, but his personal success made many of his contemporaries jealous. Eventually his persistent refusal (as Collector of Customs) to turn a blind eye to the activities of the Mayor and Corporation of Falmouth, created considerable friction within the port.

Early in 1698 a petition complaining of his abuses as Agent of Packets was presented to the House of Commons, and the matter was referred to a committee of the House of Lords. While this was progressing Gwyn was relieved of his several offices. Amongst the charges were claims that Gwyn:

- deducted one shilling in the pound from the tradesmen's

accounts, claiming that 'poundage' was a right of office
– was responsible for irregularities in the payments to lodging house keepers, who were looking after sick seamen from the packets
– was involved in underhand dealing in the disposal of 'worn out' sails and cordage from the packets
– had hired out the facilities of a government hulk anchored in Falmouth haven
– had made and received illegal shipments of salt and merchandise via the packets
– in receiving stores and provisions for the packet service, appropriated the best joints and choice items, such as the *sewett in the* Hindquarters *of* Beefe, Marabones *of* beefe, *the* Head *and* Leggs *and* Lard *of* Hoggs, *for his own use*

As Thomas Slade, a mariner serving in the **Spanish Expedition** put it, *he was ashamed to see the fraude & Abuses putt upon the Kings Majestie by the Defendants manadgeing the affaires of the Packet boats as Agent.*

Eventually Gwyn was convicted of the charges, and was fined £10,000 as well as being deprived of his several offices. Although ruined in the process, the extent of his previous success is indicated by

21

the fact that he was able to pay this swinging fine. For a short while after he served as a clerk for Francis Jones, his successor in office. But, before he could regain his former financial status, Daniel Gwyn died a result of injuries received in a fall.

Other less colourful agents followed, though several of the early ones had trouble settling their accounts with the Post Office. Both Jones, and his successor Rogers, were in arrears for several years after they ceased to hold office – though this was not then an unusual state of affairs with public accounts.

Stephen Banfield, appointed in 1723, was not from Falmouth, moving there with his family on appointment. For the next 62 years an intricate thread of nepotism ran through the service. That such conditions pertained in a close-knit community and service is not surprising, and they were considered quite acceptable by the norms of the period. From 1723 to 1785, the office of packet agent at Falmouth was held by three successive generations of one family, either by marriage or by birth. Stephen Bell succeeding to his father George in 1776, who in his turn had succeeded to his father-in-law in 1747, after having married Stephen Banfield's daughter Henrietta in 1741.

Reinforcing the ties of friends and family, Stephen Bell married Frances Lovell, the daughter of senior packet Capt Robert Lovell, of the *Prince Frederick*. His three sisters all married packet captains. His eldest daughter also married a packet commander, and his son Stephen Banfield Bell entered the packet service. Young Stephen was sailing master in acting command of the *Walsingham* (his uncle Capt Couse's command and one of the new standard packets), when she was taken prize in September 1795, only to be retaken on the 19th September off L'Orient, by the *Porcupine* frigate, and carried into Plymouth. He went on to command the *Earl of Leicester* (2), from 1803 until she too was taken prize in 1805, and was then given command of the new packet *Francis Freeling*, which he held from 1807 to the time of his death in service, in 1815.

Under Banfield and the Bells, unfettered by the strict enforcement of petty regulations, the packet service functioned freely and relatively successfully, in so far as the regular carriage of the overseas mails was concerned. However, in other respects, all was not as it should have been. Matters came to a head in 1784–5, when, as part of a larger enquiry into widespread frauds and abuses throughout the Post Office, Thomas Todd, clerk to the secretary of the Post Office, was sent to Falmouth to enquire and report. Todd found a very cosy arrangement existing between Stephen Bell and the packet commanders, all to their mutual benefit. Bell was also accused of permitting, if not actively promoting, a number of financial irregularities and was found indebted to the service in a considerable sum.

Borrowing money to try and cover this loss, he fell further into debt, and seeing no other way out, shot himself in July 1785.

In addition to the direct employees, at Falmouth and Flushing, a whole range of ancillary support services had grown up on the strength of the packet service. In direct support of the packets there were the: insurance brokers; sail-makers; block-makers; pennant and flag makers; rope-walkers; cord-winders; and riggers; chandlers; chart and stationery printers; anchor-smiths; ship surveyors; dock proprietors; shipwrights; boat-builders; ship-carpenters and sawyers; along with the innumerable boatmen, whose frail craft scuttled to and from all parts of the Fal estuary, on untold errands, servicing every need of the packets. On the provisions side there were the wholesale butchers; dairy men; poultry men; salt-provisions merchants; ships' bread and biscuit bakers; fresh produce merchants; and wine and spirit merchants. On the periphery, but inextricably linked, were the: innkeepers; hoteliers; barmaids and porters; chambermaids and pot-boys; coachmen; wagoners; farriers; harness makers; cartwrights; wheelwrights; blacksmiths; stable proprietors and forage merchants; farmers; swineherds and milkmaids. And just one step removed from them, but still drawing from the same pot, were all the other local services: builders; labourers; street-cleaners; school masters and mistresses; clergymen and ministers; shop-keepers and their assistants; tailors; hawkers and the like; magistrates and town officials; parish-overseers; gentry and land-owners, and of course, dependant on the whole, the widows and orphans; the sick and the poor.

In one way or another the whole of the neighbourhood depended on the packet service. It is impossible to be accurate as to numbers, and by the time the national census came into force, there were a host of other ships trading to and from, or calling at the port of Falmouth. However, it might not be far from the truth to suggest that for every half-a-dozen packetmen employed by the service, another two or three people were employed in one or other of the ancillary services. And, up until the appointment of Benjamin Pender in 1785, all the packet agents took some sort of cut from the income of many of these.

The abuses of the system revealed by Todd's investigations in 1784 included:

– excessive private trading by the officers and crew of the packets

– passengers travelling as the commanders' friends, avoiding the payment of the King's £4 per head

– the agent giving free passes

– irregular musters of each packets' crew, allowing packets to sail short-handed, whereby the agent pocketed the wages, and the commanders the victualling allowances, of missing hands

Francis Freeling, 1798–1836 Secretary Freeling saw through the implementation of the new working practices introduced under Todd, and established new level of personal accountability for all Post Office employees (Heritage, Royal Mail)

– payment to the agent, by the commanders, of five guineas per voyage, for managing their affairs while they were at sea. (This alone supposedly gave the Agent about £430 per annum)

– the commanders not putting to sea as soon as the mails were on board

– abuses of the commanders' private pension fund

– the abusive use of substitutes, while the commanders remained on shore on full pay

– the commanders claiming for crew, as living on board while at Falmouth, and pocketing victualling allowances

– commanders withholding the Post Office's portion of any freight on bullion

– victualling allowances paid by the Post Office for passengers, who had paid for their passage

– the agent's duties being completely unregulated

By no means all of the abuses claimed were substantiated. And, while the agent was heavily implicated, not all the commanders were deeply involved. However, the suspicions remained, and new regulations were gradually introduced to control the service and curb these excesses.

At the time of Benjamin Pender's appointment in 1785, his salary was £270 per annum. Out of that he had to pay £30 for a clerk, £10 to a postmaster, and £100 a year to Stephen Bell's widow. Leaving him with £130, the same take home salary as his predecessor. The commission of inquiry recommended that he be paid £400 per annum *and no gratuities*. That he be relieved of paying Mrs Bell her £100 pension, and that the PO pay his clerk £50 per annum. These moves were all approved, but just when they came into effect is not certain. By the end of his time as agent, his salary had been increased to £600, with increased responsibilities.

Hitherto the PMG's periodic instructions to the packet agents, had been restricted to the detail of regulating the mails, the packets, and their commanders and crew, but apart from these he was a free agent. Benjamin Pender's revised instructions now included the restrictive clause:

> *You must not be either directly or indirectly Owner in a whole or in part of any Packet Boat, nor are you or any Person under you to sell or supply any articles of Provisions or Stores whatever for the packets.*

This was the first time that these elements of insider dealing had specifically been forbidden.

The Falmouth Staff

As circumstances demanded a number of other staff were employed at Falmouth. During the war 1701–13, a *chirugen* was employed at about £200 per annum to care for the sick and wounded

*The **Francis Freeling**, 1807–1829 Named after the Post Office Secretary, this was a rare mark of honour usually reserved to Post Master Generals and above. She is portrayed off Malta in 1821, when under the command of Capt James Cunningham, and is one of six packet portraits painted by Nicholas Cammillieri, of Malta. These were recently donated to the National Maritime Museum Cornwall, by the Broad family – late shipping agents of Falmouth (NMMC)*

packet seamen at Falmouth. This surgeon was shore-based, not sea going, and the sick and hurt packetmen were lodged with families around the town. During Gwyn's agency, the accusation of having misappropriated a part of the rent of the various lodgings for sick and hurt seamen, was just one of the many charges laid against him.

As part of a later review, prior to the transfer of the service to Admiralty control in 1823, the then packet agent, Thomas Musgrove took stock of the Falmouth establishment. He reported that in addition to himself, the establishment at Falmouth consisted of the following posts:

– a searcher & inspector of packets (not to be confused with the headquarter's post) Established in 1801, partially to try and suppress smuggling on the packets, and partly to oversee the repairs and condition of the vessels. Henry Williams, the current post holder, had held the post ever since its creation. Now on an annual salary of £150, he had joined the service in 1778, and had spent ten years at sea before being appointed to his current post

– a storekeeper – date of establishment uncertain, but when Mr. Gray died in 1819, he had been succeeded by the current post holder, John Harris, on a salary of £50 per annum

– a chronometer maker. The currently post holder being William Goffe, on a salary of £150 per year, but just when the post was created was not recorded

– a collector of monies and accounts' keeper. These duties were performed by William Gay, for a salary of £50 per annum. William Gay was also Musgrove's chief clerk (which position carried its own salary of £200). Gay had been appointed clerk to Benjamin Pender in 1794, at a salary of £30. When he petitioned the PMG for an increase in 1797 he was told this was impossible, but there were subsequent increases. He served as chief clerk under Saverland, from 1810 to 1821, and under Musgrove from 1821 to 1824

In addition there were supposedly four clerks (on annual salaries ranging from £80 to £200), a messenger (on 21s per week), and four boatmen (on 2s per day each). One of these boatmen was currently substituting for a clerk, two of whom, Lott and Handes, had absconded in 1816, under suspicion of having stolen a letter containing *property*. (In 1797, Mr Lott, the Surveyor for the South West District, based at Exeter, had been sent to Falmouth *specially to instruct both the Postmaster and the person employed by him in their new duties*. These related to the receipt and dispatch of 'cross-posts', international mail sent directly to and from Falmouth, instead of going via London. Mr Lott then persuaded the PMG and Mr Pender, to accept his nephew as an additional clerk. It was

GENERAL POST-OFFICE.

July 23rd, 1816.

WHEREAS, C. J. LOTT, and J. F. HANDES, late Clerks in the Packet-Office, *Falmouth*, stand charged with Felony and have Absconded; this is to give notice, that whoever will apprehend and convict, or cause to be apprehended and convicted, both or either of the said persons, shall be entitled, on conviction, to

A REWARD OF
30 POUNDS.

The said C. J. Lott, is about 40 years of age, about 5 feet 2 inches high, light Hair, fair Complexion, and usually wears Spectacles.

And the said J. F. Handes, is about 27 years of age, about 5 feet 6 inches high, Brown Hair, and of gentlemanly appearance.

By Command of the Postmaster General,

F. FREELING, Secretary.

one of these positions that had still not be substantively filled by 1823.

Under the Admiralty it was determined that the services of the searcher, storekeeper, and chronometer maker, along with three of the boatmen, and the junior clerk were no longer required.

Although the Admiralty superintendent Capt King, RN, became responsible for the operation of the packet vessels, he had no authority for the processing of the mails. Thomas Musgrove continued as packet agent and postmaster, retaining the services of three clerks. They continued to prepare the mails for sea, and receive and sort the overseas mails prior to forwarding them to their British destinations. The release of the boatmen had to be quickly reversed, when the naval commanders stood on their dignity and refused to deliver the mails to the packet office, insisting that the PO staff come and collect them from the ship's side.

In December 1824 Musgrove was succeeded by William Gay, his chief clerk, and Pigot & Co's *Directory of Cornwall*, of about 1830, carried the following summary of the now modest packet establishment at Falmouth:

NAVAL DEPARTMENT – PACKET OFFICE, ARWENACK-STRET
W. Gay, Esq. agent – Mr. Wm. L. Drown, first clerk – Mr. J. W. Wheatley, second clerk – Mr. Wm. Gay, jun. third clerk.

William Gay continued as packet agent until 1843, when all but the Brazil packets had been replaced by private steamers carrying the mails under licence from other ports. He was then 70 years of age, having served the PO faithfully for 49 years.

The **Walsingham**, *1794-1825 One of the new 'standard' packets introduced in the 1790s. Note her three masted 'ship' rig. Cammillieri was noted for the accuracy of his ship portraits, but the people figured are all undersize – making the vessel look much bigger than she actually was. The second packet of that name, she is portrayed here in 1823 when off Malta, under the command of Lt John Bullock* (NMMC)

3 Packet Owners & Contractors

From its inception the majority of vessels employed in the Falmouth Packet Service, were privately owned craft hired from civil contractors, though the PMG insisted on naming or approving of the names of the packets. Accordingly they were the main given dignified names, that reflected their establishment status, and names associated with the Royal family proliferated throughout the service. At Falmouth, down through the 1700s, there were at least four packets named **Hanover**, three **Princess Elizabeths**, several **King Georges** along with a host of other **Queens, Princes,** and **Princesses**. At the time packets of the same name were not numbered or otherwise denoted to distinguish one from the other, but to give clarity here numbers in brackets have been added hereafter – eg. **Hanover** (3). Other packets bore the names of noble lords or their ladies, such as the **Duke of Cumberland, Earl Gower, Lady Arabella,** and **Lady Mary Pelham**. While others bore the names of prominent political figures, including a large percentage of ex Post Master Generals (many of whom were, or became, peers of the realm) – **Pitt, Walsingham, Lord Auckland, Earl of Sandwich,** and the like – or national heroes such as the **Duke of Marlborough,** or **General Wall**. Only a few bore common names such as **Mary Ann, Eliza, Snake** and **Little Catherine,** and most of the latter were temporary packets, hired at times of national emergency. To muddy the waters even more for enthusiasts trying to identify specific packets, many of these names were used concurrently by Post Office packets operating from other packet stations – Dover, Harwich and Holyhead, and later on from Yarmouth and Weymouth.

Halifax schooner

Initially there was just the one preferred contractor – Edward, or Edmund, Dummer (authorities differ in deciphering) – a man of many parts. Dummer had been appointed Surveyor General to the Navy in 1692, after just two years as Assistant Surveyor. In those capacities he designed and oversaw the initial construction of Plymouth Naval Dockyard during 1690–92. Later, in 1698, he was a co-author of A *Survey of the Ports on the South West Coast of England from Dover to the Land's End,* (along with Capt Wiltshaw – Navy Board, and Capts Conaway and Cruft – Trinity House). Amongst their findings they reported that Falmouth, in so far as its use a naval base was concerned, was *clogged with many inconvenient shoals and sudden soundings.*

In 1694, while Surveyor General to the Royal Navy, Dummer was credited with supervising the construction of a number of remarkably fast packet-boats for the PO service between Harwich and the Low Countries. Following on this success, he was asked to submit proposals for the design of packet-boats for the new Falmouth to Corunna service, as well as organising some of the operational aspects of that service.

Only sketchy details survive of the terms and conditions of Dummer's earliest contract, which took up for two packets on the Falmouth–Corunna run, about which little is known beyond their names – **Spanish Allyance** and **Spanish Expedition**. On the outbreak of war with Spain in 1701, the Iberian terminus for these packets was diverted to Lisbon, forging links that later formed the core service of the Falmouth Packet establishment. For diplomatic reasons the word 'Spanish' was then dropped from the names of these two vessels. On the Lisbon route his packets proved quite successful, though in operation they were found too big, or more to the point too expensive for the Treasury.

In June 1703, when trying to come up with a cheaper alternative, Dummer estimated the annual cost of the current service at £9,705 5s 0d. Against this he costed his revised proposals at £5,362 1s 2d, producing and estimated annual saving of £4,343 3s 10d. In the following August the PO reported to the Treasury on the state of their current negotiations. Dummer now proposed three, 160 ton vessels, each manned by 35 hands, but the PO considered that he was:

> … mistaken in calculating the charge of the boats at present made use of, the same not amounting to near as much as he computeth… His demand for 7s. 6d. per ton for wear and tear per calendar month including guns and gunner's stores seems reasonable but we cannot agree to his demand for 8 per cent. interest on the prime cost of the vessels; but we agree to a payment of 2,000l. on account as above. The Commanders of the boats are to be under the direction of the Postmasters General and of their agent at Falmouth.

In September 1703, the Treasury issued a warrant approving the new arrangements, and authorising the PMG:

> … to contract with Edward Dummer to build 3 new vessels and boats to be employed in carrying mails of letters between Falmouth and Lisbon in the room of those presently made use of in that service, and for performing the said service with the number of men and at the rates therein, he to deduct for the wages and victuals of men at any time wanting out of the complement and also to accompt for the freight of all passengers going or coming over in said boats and to have the said boats ready to begin the service at Xmas next; he to be paid 2,000l. within 3 months after the said boats shall have entered service, which sum is to be discompted out of the first annual sum payable to him hereunder: the Receiver General of the PO being to defray the charge arising by the contract for wages, victuals, wear and tear, guns and gunner's stores of the same: Dummer to render a true account of the moneys arising by freight of Passengers.

Confident of his experience and abilities, the Postal authorities were happy to deal exclusively with Dummer when a second route, to the West Indies, was proposed in 1702. As set out in a document dated June 18th of that year, for this service Dummer proposed:

– to provide four packets at 10s per *tun* per month. The Queen to victual the men, and provide guns and gunners.

— for the two biggest sloops (of 134 *tuns*) to be manned by 28 men and boys, and 12 guns each; the least two sloops (110 *tuns*) to be manned by 25 men and boys, and carry 10 guns each.

— for the Queen to reserve to herself the benefit of all letters.

— for the Queen to grant letters of marque to each vessel during war.

— for the Queen to 'protect' the men.

— that the packets wear the Queen's colours.

— that the packet contractor had the benefit of all passengers, and parcels, except letters.

— that the packets be exempt from light money and other port charges.

With all their eggs in the one basket, the PO's total reliance on a single contractor almost brought down the whole service. Ever the optimist, Dummer's arrangements had to be constantly revised, and the whole enterprise nearly failed because of shipping losses during the War of the Spanish Succession. Within a few years of opening the second service two packets on this route had been lost due to normal risks of the sea, but another seven had been taken as prizes by the enemy. Though some of the latter were returned on payment of a ransom, the strain on the West India service was so severe that it had to be prematurely terminated towards the end of 1711. The last packet sailing on this service being the **Martlett**, which set out on the 20th July, returning to Tenby, on the 19th December.

The close of the War of the Spanish Succession in 1713, removed any pressing need for the Government to resurrect this service. Peacetime communications with the West Indies could be adequately handled by ship mail – that is mail carried by any occasional ship that happened to be sailing that way.

The Postal authorities learnt by their experience, and began to spread their risks by negotiating a number of single packet contracts against a framework of standard terms and conditions. The second generation of packet contractors were a bit of a mixed bag, but mainly consisted of established merchant shipowners. Throughout the PO held a right to veto captains in command of the packets, but quite quickly a number of packet commanders acquired sufficient wealth or security to finance their own vessels, at least in partnership, if not in outright sole ownership. This was a growing trend, and as the century progressed the number of packet-owning commanders increased dramatically.

Ships were legally property, and for share ownership a packet ship (as were all other merchant ships of the period) comprised 64 equal shares, though for everyday convenience these might be reduced to lesser common multiples. Each legal owner held a proportionate number of the 64 shares, which could be retained, bequeathed, mortgaged, sold or assigned, as with any other real-estate property. In addition to owning shares in their own command, many packet commanders also took up shares in other packets as a form of mutual insurance, and a number of other sub-contractors to the packet service also acquired shares in one or more packets, as a side investment. When the Exeter carrier Robert Russell died in 1823, his shares in six Falmouth packets were offered for sale. His packet holdings consisting of, one-quarter of John Bull's **Duke of Marlborough** (2), one-eighth of the packets **Montagu**, and **Countess of Chichester**, and one-sixteenth part of the **Duke of Kent** (2), **Lord Hobart**, and the **Francis Freeling**. During the early years of the service there is a strong suggestion that some of the packet agents at Falmouth, and at least one PMG, also held shares in the packets. A practice that was not specifically forbidden until the 1790s.

By the early 1720s the Falmouth Packet Service had reached a degree of maturity that made it almost self-regulating. Procedural customs and practices were firmly established, and the service contracts had been formalised and structured to meet nearly every conceivable eventuality. Established contractors now had a firm grip on the service, and while their contracts formally came up for renewal every three years or so, there were relatively few new entrants to the service. Four packets now provided the core Lisbon service – **King George** (1), **Expedition** (3), **Prince Frederick** (1), and **Hanover** (1).

When, during the War of the Austrian Succession (1740–48), it was decided in July 1743 to re-establish a packet service to the West Indies , the PO reviewed the terms of Dummer's earlier contract. By this he had provided four or five packets, of 140 tons, each manned by 26 hands, at an annual cost of £12,000. The PO now proposed to contract for four boats of 100 tons, each manned by 28 hands, for £8,372 per annum. It was hoped that this cost would be offset by the income from the postage on letters to and from the West Indies. During the last war these had stood at about £5,000 per annum, and were now assumed to have increased significantly. Exactly when this service was re-instituted is not certain. Unfortunately no surviving contracts have been found from this period, nor yet many contemporary packet-letters either. However, shipping records show that four packets were running more or less regularly to the West Indies between 1746 and 1749 – **Swallow** (1), **Eagle** (2) **Countess of Leicester** (1) and **Fawkener** (1).

From time to time contractors tried to get the better of the PO, while the PO constantly tried to secure the best possible service at the lowest effective cost. In this the Treasury frequently tried to push them towards the cheapest contractor, with scant regard as to how well they might or might not fulfil the terms of their contracts. As a result of such pressure, as new routes were added to the Falmouth Station, packets of different sizes were specified: 145–150 tons, to the West Indies in 1755; 130 tons, New York in 1755; and 170 tons, West Indies in 1766.

Each service was covered by a set of contracts, but as the hire terms were originally based on the actual tonnage of the packets, it was only natural for the contractors to try and get as large a vessel as possible approved. Accordingly the packets supplied by the contractors were often larger than specified, but any profiteering from this practice was eliminated in the 1750s, when the PO hire rates were set to the approved tonnage for each service. In addition to rates of hire, a set of basic terms and conditions (specific to each service route) were applied to each packet, setting their wartime and peacetime established compliments, rates of pay, victualling allowances, etc.

In November 1755 the PO signed a seven-year West India contract (for some reason with only one pair of contractors – Richard Stratton and John Sargent), to provide four packets. As specified these were to be of 150 tons each, manned by 16 officers and men, and armed with eight carriage guns and six swivel guns. The hire rate was equivalent to £171 10s each per lunar month – £2,229 10s per annum. From contemporary shipping reports these four were the **Duke**, **Earl of Newcastle**, **Lady Augusta**, and **Fawkener** (2). The latter may or may not have been the same vessel as the earlier **Fawkener**, but in July 1759 it was agreed that her commander, John James (or Jones), be allowed £100 for the gallant defence ... *on the 7th April last when he was attacked by a large French Sloop of twelve carriage guns and upwards of one hundred men, between Barbadoes and Antigua.*

Thereafter the PO mainly stuck to single packet contracts. However, towards the end of the 1770s they were persuaded to supply their own packets, cutting out the middlemen in a vain hope of reducing costs. This move is covered more fully in a later chapter, but it proved an expensive failure, and in the early 1790s, they relinquished this idea for once and for all.

Following the 1785 enquiry into the frauds and abuses in the PO, a standard design 179 ton packet, was approved for use on all routes, and all the old style packets were to be released as soon as their replacements could be built. Twenty-two or three of these standard packets were to be built by 1800, and partly to establish the bona fides of the initial design concept, and partly as a result of their earlier self-ownership policy, the first three were built at the direct cost of the PO. These building costs later being recovered from their commander/owners during their early years in service.

Despite this notional standard, individual packet contractors, or commanders had strong opinions on what was best for them. Invariably there was an element of bigger is better, but this tendency was restrained by strict financial penalties being imposed whenever the design constraints were exceeded beyond reasonable limits. In 1801, two new packets – Capt Blight's **Lord Chesterfield** (2), and Capt Bull's **Duke of Marlborough** (1) – were both found to be considerably oversize. Capt John Bull's new packet, was nearly 40 tons bigger than the stipulated 179 tons, but after lengthy discussions the PMG ruled that both packets could be admitted into the service, on the proviso that they:

> *... so long as they may severally remain in our Service, shall at the Expence of the respective Commanders carry an additional Complement of Men, in the settled Proportions of Peace and War for all the Tonnage of their Vessels above the Establishment of 179 tons.*

By which proviso captains Blight and Bull found themselves having to employ four extra seamen each, at an additional cost to themselves of about £140 a year.

The normal contract procedures stood the service in good stead, except in times of war. War placed innumerable strains on the service, not least in that it was usually under wartime conditions that new packet routes were pioneered. New routes required additional packets just when packet losses were already abnormally high due to enemy action. Such a high level of demand required extraordinary measures to make good the shortfall. These took the form of temporary contracts, whereby vessels well below the normal packet specification were admitted into the service. Whereas the standard contracts ran for three or more years, the temporary contracts were limited to six months certain, or twelve months certain. The shorter term attracting a higher rate, but with no guarantee of continued hire beyond the minimum period agreed. However, such was the demand for packets through the Napoleonic and American wars that many temporary contracts ran for years on end. To try and prevent these temporary contracts from totally subverting the terms and standing of the regular packets, standard contracts were modified to include even higher rates for war service, and a number of temporary allowances, outside the strict terms of the contracts, were tolerated.

The wartime establishment included higher manning levels, allowances for arms and ammunition, as well as payment of a pre-determined sum for total loss by enemy action, and pro-rata for damage repair. In theory this compensation was sufficient to enable the contractor/owners to finance a replacement vessel, when wartime insurance cover became prohibitive, and thus reduce any potential disruption to the service. However, it occasionally failed to achieve this aim in practice. When in September 1798, Capt Dodd was still a prisoner in France – following the capture of his packet **Countess of Leicester** (2), by the French privateer **L'Insurgent**, on December 10th, 1797: Francis Freeling was forced to acknowledge: H*is friends here I fear are not competent to hire a Temporary Vessel or to build one.*

Xebec off Gibralter 1780

4 The Falmouth Packets & their development to the 1790s

Cutter

The first two packets employed on the Falmouth station were unable to maintain the service schedule to and from the Groyne of Corunna, and the hire of two additional packets was reluctantly approved by the Treasury. The **Prince**, commanded by Zachary Rogers, joined the **Spanish Allyance** and **Spanish Expedition** towards the end of January 1689, but the fourth packet has not been positively identified. Contrary to Treasury hopes, the early service was not self financing, and they demanded economies. On July 27th, 1700, a Treasury warrant was issued to the Postmaster General authorising them to:

> ... *establish vessels of about 90 or 100 tons with 10 or 12 men each to go from Falmouth to the Groyne; to be paid as formerly out of the PO revenue: all in order to the safe and regular conveyance of his Majesty's letters between England and Spain by vessels of sufficient force to make defence against the ordinary privateers...*

It is not known if any of these smaller packets were brought into commission on this service, nor how they were going to be of *sufficient force*. The later **King William**, was of this size, but she was placed on the West India run. The vessels described seem too small to have effectively fulfilled the service, and in 1703 Dummer, the packet contractor, suggested that three 160 tons packets, manned by 35 hands *may perform that service very well* ... By then the Iberian terminal had been diverted to Lisbon, and the service was maintained by four sloops, one pair of 134 tons each, carrying 12 guns and manned by 38 men and boys, together with a second pair of 110 tons each – 10 guns and 35 crew.

For the new monthly service to the West Indies, Dummer first proposed four packets of 140 tons, each manned by 26 men. Other than for pure economy, there seems no logical reason why smaller packets should have been considered suitable for the West India service. Whatever, the new service commenced with the **Bridgeman** clearing from the Needles on October 21st 1702, and taking 104 days to complete her first round voyage.

There were now ostensibly eight Falmouth packets – four on the Lisbon run – **Allyance** (Capt Green), **Expedition** (Clies), **Prince** (1) (Rogers) – renamed **Six Islands** in 1704/5 and **Queen** (Culverton) and four on the West Indies run – **Bridgeman** (unknown), **Mansbridge** (Chenall), **King William** (Smith) and a second **Prince** (2) (also unknown).

Early losses, replacements and name changes, quickly cloud this picture, and there were operational headaches caused by the West India packets returning to different British ports spread between Plymouth and Liverpool. As first conceived, the service schedule for the West Indies route allowed 90 days for the round voyage, Falmouth to Falmouth, including stopovers of 21 days at the different ports of call. This was revised to allow 100 days for the round voyage, with stopovers of $19\frac{1}{2}$ days, allowing 20 to 30 days at Falmouth to refit and prepare for the next voyage. In practice even this schedule proved impossible to maintain. The average voyage, during the first couple of years, was about 112 days, with both the shortest and the longest round voyages being made by the **Mansbridge** – 92 and 116 days respectively.

With operational experience it quickly became apparent that four packets could not maintain a monthly service to the West Indies, and in 1705 a new contract was drawn up authorising five larger packets – **Queen Anne**, **Jamaica**, **Barbadoes**, **Prince George** and **Antigoe**. Progressively brought into service from June 1705, these were two decked ships of about 200 tons burthen. As a sweetener Dummer was allowed to carry five tons of freight outwards, and ten tons homeward. Large by previous standards, these packets were fitted with 24 sweeps, for rowing when becalmed, and for defensive armament they carried 20 carriage guns, with a corresponding manning level. Most of the guns were carried on the lower, or main deck, leaving the upper deck free for working the ship. Unfortunately these packets had so little freeboard that most of the gun-ports were frequently awash, and heeling in a stiff breeze was sufficient to rendered the mid-ships guns unserviceable, a factor which severely effected their defensive capabilities.

The first ten years of the 18th century were indeed turbulent times and there is much confusion as to what happened to individual packets. A confusion that was aggravated by the emerging practice of re-using packet names. The original **Allyance**, was *cast away in the mouth of the river at Lisbon by striking on a sand bar which had been shifted by violent storms and a land flood…*, in February 1707(8). Previously, in 1707, the new **Allyance** had been taken prize *…in her outward voyage… by 2 French privateers, each of much superior force, after a very sharp engagement with them both for above 8 hours.* In the following May, salvaged and repaired, the old **Allyance**, was re-commissioned under a Capt Hooper.

The **Expedition**, under Capt Clies, was ordered to be sold in September 1704, when her commander was suspended for making disloyal remarks about the Royal family. She was replaced by the **Mansbridge**, under Capt John Chenall, which having started out on the Gravesend to Brill service, was diverted to the West India service, and then put onto the Lisbon run, only to be taken prize by the French in February 1704(5). The old **Expedition** was brought back into service under the command of Capt Francis Clies Junior, son of her former commander. He and his crew beat off a heavy attack when off the Scillies in February 1705(6), when the old **Expedition**, was described as:

> … *carrying 26 guns and a crew of 90 and commanded by young Capt Clyes who did his duty very well a few months ago against an enemy privateer stronger than he, which had attacked him in sight of the Scilly Islands: he*

forced the privateer to stand out to sea, having killed 50 of his men and wounded 80 with his guns firing case-shot as has appeared since by news from France. Capt Clyes was wounded in the head, but did not give up the command of his ship, and he came very well out of the affair.

This was one of the earliest accounts of packetmen's bravery, but despite her proven fighting ability, she was taken prize in March 1707(8). A new boat, the **Godolphin**, commanded by Capt Gibson was built in 1705, only to be carried into St. Malo as a prize in January 1705(6). Another short-lived packet, the **Lisbon**, had been taken prize in December 1704, and the **Queen** was also taken – her ex-commander being a prisoner of war at Dinan in 1706.

The first West India service was suspended just before the close of the War of the Spanish Succession, and with the peace it was allowed to lapse. Only four packets now remained in the PO's service, those on the Lisbon run. One of the established Lisbon packets was the **Hanover**, a name which appears to have been introduced in 1712, in loyal flattery of the House of Hanover, anticipating George I's succession in 1714. Some idea of the confusion caused by the long-term reuse of a name for generations of successive packets can be gained from reviewing the history of the several **Hanovers**.

A **Hanover** was contracted to the PO for three years by her owner and commander, Henry Osborne, in August 1722. She had already served at least one contract term as an established Lisbon packet, and she seems to be the **Hanover** of 1712 – **Hanover** (1). A 120-ton vessel, hired at the rate of £75 per lunar month, she was manned by 15 Able Seamen besides the Commander. Her contract specifies no other officers, and she appears to have served up until 1741 when she was laid up and replaced by a new packet of the same name.

Hanover (2) was a Thames built vessel of 150 tons, a little bigger than her predecessor, and rigged as a snow. She was jointly owned by Thomas Strickland of Woolnoth, London, and Anthony Todd and Philip Enouf. Todd and Enouf were both established packet captains resident at Falmouth – Todd commanding the **Expedition** (2), while Enouf, a former Channel Islander, had command of the **Hanover** (2). In 1743, as a Roman Catholic, he'd had to swear an oath *for preventing the Dangers which may happen from Popish Recusants*. In 1754 command of **Hanover** (2) passed to one Williams, and Enouf retired – becoming High Sheriff of Cornwall in 1762.

Joseph Sherburn, the next commander of the **Hanover** (2), was commissioned on September 15th, 1755. On the outbreak of the Seven Years War, she was provided with 14 carriage guns of unknown poundage, but these proved insufficient, and she was taken prize by a French privateer and carried into Brest in March 1757. Sherburn and his crew appear not to have been repatriated until some months later, but a **Hanover** (3) was running in her stead within weeks.

Hanover (3) remains something of an enigma. Sailing at first under Williams, with Sherburn taking command from February 2nd 1758, she had a brief career as a Lisbon packet, which closed with her tragic wreck in December 1763, off the north coast of Cornwall, near St. Agnes.

In recent years attempts to salvage 'treasure' from the wreck of the **Hanover** (3) have brought her some notoriety. Much has been made of the merchants' treasure on board, waiting to be salvaged. Current research reveals that, within days of her loss, many loose gold coins were recovered from the sands at low tide. Determined attempts to recover the treasure chest proved at first ineffective. Contemporary estimates of the value of the chest's contents varied from £16,000 to £60,000. Over a year later, and some time after the insurance had been paid on the loss, the bullion chest was recovered intact. Sent to London unopened, in April 1765, it was found on arrival to contain 20,000 moidores, then worth about £27,000. With the recovery of the chest intact, there is little evidence to suggest that any substantial amount of treasure now remains on the wreck site. The ship's bell and a few representative items salvaged from the wreck site feature in the Packet Gallery, at the National Maritime Museum Cornwall.

A little over a year after **Hanover** (3) was commissioned, **Hanover** (2) – now sailing as a French naval advice-boat under the name **Duc de Hanovre** or **L'Hanovre** (again contemporary accounts differ) – was retaken by HM ships **Lizard** and **Hampshire**. After being regularly condemned as a prize of war, she was advertised for sale *by the Candle, at the Star-Tavern, Plymouth, on Friday the 6th of April, 1759...* Her subsequent fate has yet to be discovered.

A **Hanover** (4) appeared on the run within days of **Hanover** (3)'s loss in December 1763, but she appears to have been a temporary packet, sailing under the command of one Copland (or Coplin), for only two voyages before command passed to a different Capt Anthony Todd in March 1764. He was probably a son of the earlier Anthony Todd, who'd held a stake in **Hanover** (2) – and presumably in numbers three, four and five, as well. In July 1764, Todd brought down a new **Hanover** (5), just built on the Thames. He commanded her for 22 years in the Lisbon service, before retiring on a pension of £150 per annum in 1786. When the packets were being armed in November 1776, because of the American War of Independence, she had been described as a ship of 230 tons, and *in good shape*.

On Todd's retirement, command of **Hanover** (5) passed to his son Lovell Todd. Only 19 at the time, Lovell Todd was a reluctant sailor, and while he retained nominal command of her until she was replaced by the **Prince of Wales** in 1796, he frequently remained on shore leaving her under the temporary command of his sailing master, Harris. Withdrawn from the service towards the end of 1796, **Hanover** (5) was offered for sale in January 1797, and again in the following May. With her retirement the name of **Hanover** disappeared from the annals of the Falmouth Packet Service.

Bending to Treasury pressure, in the early 1780s the PO became owners of a number of packets – being persuaded that they could run them more cheaply than the hired packets. They could not! In all thirteen or fourteen packets came under PO ownership between 1779 and 1798, and two of them proved very costly failures. These were not of the normal run of packets, but larger experimental vessels. Commissioned in August 1779, the **Speedy** (1) (D'Auvergne), and **Swift** (Nichols), were of 310 tons each, well armed and manned to test the West India merchants' assertions that such packets would be better able to defend themselves. Although not quite lost on their first voyage, as later noted by Francis Freeling, they did not last very long. In May 1782, after less than three years in the service, they were dispatched together for the West Indies – **Speedy** (1) for Jamaica and the **Swift** for the Leeward Islands. Travelling in company for mutual protection, they were approaching the Windward Islands, when, as her Surgeon and two gentlemen passengers later revealed to the *Cornwall Chronicle & Jamaica General Advertiser*:

> ... on the evening of the 15th July, they were in sight of Barbadoes, when they discovered two large frigates, close under the land, by which they were both shortly after captured, after having thrown the guns overboard and made some other fruitless attempts to escape.
>
> The frigates were the French King's ships **La Friponne**, of 44 guns and 350 men, and **Le Resolu**, of 40 guns and 330 men.
>
> The packets were conducted to Guadeloupe, from whence they were to be fitted out as corvettes.

By this account they were on their normal course, approaching Barbados from the east. A course largely dictated by the north-east trade winds, and which was quite predictable, having been followed for generations. Over the years a number of packets were taken prize during their final approach to Barbados, but even so this approach course continued to be used right up to the last days of the sailing packets.

It has been suggested that the commanders, hoping to exploit the size and armament of their vessels, deviated from their course in search of easy prizes among the inter-island traders. But the facts do not support this suggestion, and Edward D'Auvergne remained in favour with the PO, being restored to command of the **Speedy** (1) when she was retaken in 1783. He later acquired one of the new standard packets, the **Carteret** (3), when completed in August 1792, but left the service in the following year.

These two packets had cost the PO about £8,500 each, and represented a significant loss when considered against the £4,000 to

£5,000 for a standard packet. As indicated the **Speedy** (1) was fortunately recaptured, recovering some of that loss. Even so, they represented a costly experiment that was not repeated.

The PO dropped the idea of owning their own packets early in 1790 (though it was some years before they were all sold or disposed of), and a new class of hired packets, of 179 tons built to a standard design was adopted. These were to be lightly armed swift sailing vessels, able to use their speed to keep out of trouble. They were to avoid action at all costs. The design of the new standard packets allowed greater flexibility in their use, along with a rationalisation of marine stores and replacement spars, each offering great economies. No longer were packets restricted to particular service routes, and with the exception of the more lucrative Lisbon service, which remained the domain of the senior commanders, all other routes were open to the first packet available, with the senior commander taking his pick when two or more packets were at Falmouth, ready for service.

To promote the new design, the PO placed the orders for the first two or three new design packets with Marmaduke Stalkart, a Thames shipbuilder, while another two were placed with Mr Yorke at Garnett, Randall & Brent's yard in Rotherhithe. These packets cost around £3,200 each – ready for sea, and while still under construction the PO decided that they should be sold on to their new commanders. Among the first of this class completed were **Carteret** (3), **Westmoreland**, **Princess Royal**, **Princess Augusta** (2) and **Duchess of York**. As an experiment, the first two were fitted with Gottlieb's Perpetual Logs. These devices were built into the hull of the packets, with an external impeller, set deep below the water line, connected to a recording device within the ship. These logs were designed to give continuous readings of the distance travelled through the water, and by calculation an indication of speed. Costing around £40 each, they proved unreliable, and were not adopted for general use.

These standard packets formed the basis of the new class that, with only a modest increase in size during the early 1800s, gave sterling service until replaced by naval brigs from 1823.

5 Packet Commanders

Lugger 1790

In general the packet commanders were flamboyant characters with strong personalities. Prominent members of the community, they were men of some style, cutting a dash in fine uniforms. With a number of regular naval officers living in the locality, the place *literally sparkled with gold epaulets, gold lace hats, and brilliant uniforms*. As there was no official packet service uniform the commanders assumed a style of uniform dress that was barely distinguishable from those worn by Royal Naval officers. This practice caused annoyance in naval circles – as did the uniforms of the officers in the Honourable East India Company. In October 1787, in response to a query from the PMG, the Secretary to the Admiralty was instructed:

> ... *for the information of the Post Master General that if the Button holes on their Uniforms be embroidered with silver instead of Gold & the Buttons of white metal instead of being gilt, My Lords are of opinion it will sufficiently distinguish the Difference in the Uniform...*

Several half pay naval lieutenants, fully entitled to wear the king's uniform, also command some of the packets, which only added to the confusion. As a group they all enjoyed a social standing superior to the normal run of small merchant ship commanders. Constituted Master and Commander by Admiralty warrant, they were accorded the honorific title of Captain.

During that long period of almost perpetual war from 1775 to

Kempthorne House, Flushing
These substantial houses line the northern side of St Peter's Road. Originally known as the New Road, before the trees matured they enjoyed panoramic views over the packet moorings in Falmouth harbour. Very handy for the ship-building and repair yards at Little Falmouth, many were occupied by packet captains
No4 – William Kempthorne, c1786, & Richard Dodd c1799
No5 – Edward Yescombe, c1785, and later Sir Edward Pellew
No7 – John Bull after his first marriage in 1799
No9 – Henry Blight, c1789

Marlborough House
John Bull's imposing
residence built after his
second marriage.
Originally called
Marlborough Cottage,
after his packet, a
second story was later
added to the two single
story wings and the
name changed to
Marlborough House.
Note the marble plaque
of Bull's packet on the
central gable end

1815, Falmouth became a fashionable watering place, though *The greater
number of the captains and officers of those packets, as well as most of their crews,
lived ... at Flushing.*

The commanders' standing in the community was reflected by
their housing. As was the fashion of those times, most packet captains
leased their residences, and in the main they occupied superior
housing stock. These properties were frequently advertised, when
tenancies were relinquished, and such adverts give an insight into their
size, style and mode of furnishing.

In 1798 Edward Yescombe, part owner and commander of the
King George (4), was in possession of Great Wood, a fine estate in the
parish of Mylor, *where the sea flows round*. For a time, on his marriage to
Susannah Peters in October 1793, he had leased one of a row of houses
in New Road, Flushing (a very popular location with packet
commanders and sea captains). Soon after he acquired the lease to the
adjoining property, presumably linking them to form one dwelling.
Then, upwardly mobile, he moved on to Great Wood.

John Bull, who was to command three packets during his career,
married Phillipa Powel, *a young lady who, to the possession of a genteel fortune,
adds the most endearing manners, and every amiable quality that can render the
marriage state truly happy*, in May 1799. They too went to live at New Road,
Flushing, in No. 7. After Phillipa's death in 1807, John moved over to
Falmouth, possibly living with his father or brother. Some years later he
married Phoebe Marshall in Lisbon, and brought her home to newly

Dunstanville Terrace, Falmouth
This elevated terrace of fine Georgian houses, overlooks Falmouth harbour and the anchorage. Dating from the early 1800s, they were built by the Bassett estate in a partially successful bid to woo the packet commanders away from Flushing

built Marlborough Cottage. Named after his packet, Marlborough Cottage overlooked a handsome estate of 30 acres, with vistas over Swanpool and Falmouth bay, to the Manacles and the Lizard peninsula beyond.

The Green Bank area of Falmouth was also to prove attractive to those commanders not wishing to live across the water in Flushing. As part of a general development plan, in May 1801 the Bassett Estate released land for building superior houses at Green Bank – the Bassett's of Tehidy then owning extensive tracts of land throughout Cornwall. While the proposed quay works and harbour were never constructed, an elegant terrace of waterside houses was completed and duly named Dunstanville Terrace – Sir Francis Bassett being created Baron de Dunstanville in 1796. This terrace with its elevated promenade remains a charming feature of the Falmouth waterfront. Amongst these houses were properties occupied by William Dashwood – late commander of several packets, and another for his brother-in-law and fellow commander, Charles Couse, *recently of the* **Walsingham** (2).

The property occupied by Capt William Dorset Fellowes, commander of the ill-fated **Lady Hobart**, came on the market following his preferment to a Holyhead packet post. While his wife was closing the house he went on one last voyage in his packet, and was lucky to survive her tragic loss after striking an iceberg.

While the packet commanders lived in some style, and enjoyed a lively social life, they were not necessarily the most welcome tenants. In May 1830, Stephen Doble, the Bailiff at Trefusis, wrote concerning potential new tenants ... *for God's sake don't let it to a Captain of a Packet, as the men coming and going to the house breaking down all before them, will make me mad.*

Packet commanders, if not already substantial men of means, were, with a little luck and a following wind, able to acquire modest wealth during their time in the packet service. Prominent amongst their number were men such as, Capt Roberts, who served in the Falmouth Packets for 36 years, 32 of them in command. Between 1779 and 1812, a most turbulent period, he commanded four different packets – **Dashwood** (2), 1779–95; **Princess Elizabeth** (1), 1795–97; the temporary packet **Harlequin**, 1797–1800; and **Walsingham** (2), 1800–12. Britain was at war for 24 of those 32 years, and his second command, the **Princess Elizabeth** (1), was one of that new class of packets supposed to be able show a clean pair of heels to any attacker. Unfortunately, like so many others, she failed in this respect. In February 1797, after less than two years in service, she was taken prize while homeward bound from Martinique. Roberts, a third generation packets-man, survived this incident and went on to become the senior commander in 1808/9, serving on the Lisbon run for a little over three years before retiring in 1812.

Already mentioned was Capt John Bull, that larger than life, plain speaking, bluff, archetypal British sea dog. His full story is told in that admirable book of the same name, by Commander John Beck. Bull was probably a third generation packetman. His father James went on to enjoy a long and honourable retirement, but Samuel (relationship uncertain) was lost with the rest of his crew when the **Earl of Shelburn**, foundered on Nantucket Shoals in March 1786. During 45 years in the service, Capt John Bull held command of three packets – **Grantham**, 1798–1800; **Duke of Marlborough**, 1802–04; and a second **Duke of**

Windsor & Montague, Dunstanville Terrace, Falmouth
Two of the more imposing houses built at the western end of this terrace. Named after two of the Falmouth packets, they were probably originally occupied by their respective commanders

Marlborough, 1806–32. Though wounded on several occasions, he survived a number of skirmishes with the enemy, together with one spirited engagement with a Royal Navy sloop, to enjoy a measure of prosperity and nearly 20 years of retirement. John Bull is mentioned in later chapters, but two incidents will perhaps illustrate his bluff nature.

John Bull was the proud possessor of a silver toothpick stand, in the form of a pig. During one of the many rummages of his packet by the customs officers, this pig was (quite incorrectly) seized as contraband. John duly attended the custom house auction sale of seized property, and when his pig came up declaimed *Damme! That's my pig!* In the stir of the moment, no one bid against him, and it was knocked down to him for threepence.

Towards the end of his career John Bull allegedly declined a knighthood. As he put it to his second wife, *I am plain John Bull, and I shall be plain John Bull until I die!* But *I should be Lady Bull*, protested his wife. *Lady Devil!* he is alleged to have replied.

On the other hand there was unlucky Capt John Servante. Prior to joining the packet service, while serving as a Lieutenant on HMS **Juno** (32 guns), he had suffered a dreadful accident in which both his thighs were smashed by a flailing mainsheet block. The accident occurring off Weymouth (where the Royal Family were then on holiday), their Majesties took an active interest in his welfare. Placed under the personal care of his Majesty's physician, Servante made a fair recovery, but was found unfit for further active naval service. Accordingly King George III settled a pension on him and recommended him to the PMG for a packet command.

Appointed to command the old, PO owned packet **Roebuck** in 1794, by July 1795 he had already spent nine months ashore due to ill

46

*John Bull
(1772–1851)
Probably the best
known of all the
packet commanders,
this portrait shows
him in his prime, and
well illustrates his
bluff, no nonsense,
character
(Mrs Horsford)*

health. He was however in command when the **Roebuck** was taken prize on March 23rd 1798, by **L'Adelaide**, a French privateer of 16 guns – after having duly thrown the mail overboard. The packet was in turn re-taken on April 1st by the **Nimrod** and **Lurcher**, Royal Navy cutters, 20 leagues north west of Cape Ortegal, near the port Ferrol, on the coast of Northern Spain. First purchased by the PO in 1780, for use as a pool packet the **Roebuck** had suffered hard usage at the hands of a succession of commanders. By 1798 she was quite old, tired and heavy, and was now sold to clear her salvage costs.

Servante and his crew were soon repatriated, and meanwhile a new private packet had been under construction at Mr. T. Dunsterville's yard at Devil's Point, Plymouth. Servante was given command of her, and she was launched on May 1st 1798, as the **Duke of York** (2). Only a few months later the west country newspaper *Sherborne Mercury*, of Monday, September 3rd 1798, reported:

> *Falmouth, August 30 – The* **Duke of York** *packet boat, Capt. Servante, which sailed from hence about 8 weeks since, with the mail for Jamaica, was captured a few days after she sailed by a French privateer of 20 guns. This account was brought last night by the steward of the packet, who was released, together with the passengers, by the captain of the privateer. The* **Duke of York** *is quite a new vessel, this being her first voyage.*

Just five days out on her maiden voyage she had been taken

prize by **La Confiance**, a French Privateer working out of Bordeaux, and carried into Passages in Spain. This loss cost the PO £3,732 4s 6d in compensation to her owners, who appear to have included Servante in their number.

Again imprisoned for a short time, Capt Servante was duly exchanged for a French a prisoner of war, and on his *return from captivity* he placed an order for another new packet. Again she was to be built at Plymouth by Dunsterville, and as was the custom, Capt Servante was given leave to oversee her construction. Heavy losses to the enemy were placing a great strain on the packet service, and the PMG was constantly urging Servante (and others) to hurry along the building work. To which he asserted that he *could not get one built in less than two years and five months*, during the whole of which time his personal supervision was given to the work. A later edition of the *Naval Chronicle* records that she was launched by moonlight on February 13th 1801.

She too was named **Duke of York** (3), and was delivered to Falmouth just under two months later, on April 3rd. After the completion of her final outfit, and taking in her sea-stock, the new packet set out on her maiden voyage to Jamaica on May 12th. It hardly seems possible, but Capt Servante's long string of bad luck now turned worse! In August 1801, while at Jamaica awaiting the homeward mails, he was struck down with the dreaded yellow fever, and died. The fever was then virulent in the island, and four members of his crew also died on the homeward passage, together with two passengers.

Some months after Capt Servante's death his household effects were put up for auction at his Green Bank home. The inclusion in the inventory of *a Stream Cable, some coils of Rope, a Main Yard, and other Ship Stores*, highlights the fact that commanders' homes, frequently included storage for spare ship's gear.

As previously remarked, seniority in the Falmouth Packet Service carried preferment to the lucrative Lisbon service, which was the preserve of the senior four or five commanders. Their current position on the 'list' was a constant preoccupation for most junior commanders. Capt John Bull noted on the death of John Servante in 1801 – while regretting that he had, … *left a widow and eleven or twelve small children, all girls*. He could not help adding … *it brings me nearer the Lisbon station, only four above me*.

As we have seen with Capt Servante, influence and patronage played a significant part in the appointment of some commanders. Another was Thomas Patrickson Braithwaite, *a rough seaman of Herculean proportions*, who had served as flag lieutenant under Lord Howe, during the Seven Years War (1755–63). Possibly wounded, he appears to have joined the packet service, before the close of the war. After only a few voyages as master, he was established as a commander in July 1763, when appointed to the brand new packet **Hampden** (2) — then under completion on the Thames. Patronage is suspected because of his rapid rise in the service, and the fact that he almost immediately became a senior commander, appointmed to the coveted Lisbon service. Braithwaite served with some distinction for 30 years, though there were blemishes on his career. He retired due to ill health about the end of 1793, only to die a few months later on April 3rd 1794. A renowned private trader, in 1785 Braithwaite was alleged to have imported goods in excess of £40,000, when he was charged with being engaged *in compromising transactions in Brazil.* Charged with him was Crease, his sailing master, and together they went into hiding, while the **Hampden** (2), was laid up for the latter part of that year.

After the dust had settled, the two fugitives surrendered, and were sent to London, but nothing more is known about this matter. Both men returned to the service, and the **Hampden** (2) recommenced her regular Lisbon runs on November 6th 1785.

Just a handful of seamen were able to rise through the ranks of the packet service to become commanders, though their ultimate preferment usually hung on some act of distinction. Such men were John Watkins, Master of the packet **Montagu** at the time of the notorious **Globe** action, and William Rogers, whose life story reads like a Hornblower novel.

In 1795, at the age of 17, Rogers embarked in the PO packet **Countess of Leicester** (1), only to find himself made a prisoner of war when she was captured by the French frigate **L'Insurgente**, on October 12th 1797. Fortunately he was amongst a batch of prisoners exchanged in June 1798, and on his return to Falmouth he joined the packet **Carteret** (3), but

Mr William Rogers As sailing master in temporary command of the packet **Windsor Castle**, *he and his crew not only beat off an attacking privateer, but turned the tables on them, taking them prize*

The **Countess of Chichester**, 1809-30 Command of this packet was first given to Capt Rogers as part of his reward for his gallant action on board the **Windsor Castle** in 1807, when the French privateer **Le Jeune Richard** was taken prize. She is portrayed here under a later commander, Capt William Kirkness, entering Malta on July 6th 1817 (NMMC)

alas she too was taken prize while homeward bound from Jamaica in March 1800. This time Rogers was only imprisoned for three months before he was again exchanged.

After release he sailed in the packet **Duke of Clarence**, only to be captured a third time when she was taken by a Spanish privateer in December 1800. Carried into Tenerife, her captain, surgeon and steward were quickly exchanged and arrived at Plymouth in mid-March on board a Swedish brig, but the rest of the crew were held prisoner for some time. Rogers, however, managed to escape and returned home aboard an American ship.

Arriving at Falmouth in May 1801, he resumed his career, serving briefly on board the temporary packet **Penelope**, before transferring to the **Duke of Kent** (1) in the following year. Once again he lingered for a spell in a French prison after an encounter with another French ship, the **Sans Pareil** in May 1804, only to be released four months later.

On his return to Falmouth in September 1804, William Rogers joined the new packet, **Windsor Castle**. Now aged 26, and having attained the rank of sailing master, Rogers was given temporary command of the **Windsor Castle** whenever her regular commander took leave. On a Leeward Island voyage at the end of August 1807, as they approached Barbados the packet was chased by a French privateer **Le Jeune Richard** (or **La Genii** – whichever). On closing with the packet, the French commander demanded in *very opprobrious language* (as Rogers expressed it) that the **Windsor Castle** should strike. Rogers replied that she would, *and pretty hard*, as he vigorously set about engaging his attacker.

An account of this action appears in the introduction, and many others have been published. Sufficient to say here that Rogers and his crew were triumphant, and not only repelled every attempt to take his packet, but also captured their attacker. By the close of action, the **Windsor Castle** was left with only 16 of her crew of 28 unhurt, and the privateer with only 30 men. Rogers and his crew had taken the crack French schooner of Guadeloupe, and had killed or seriously injured 56 of her crew. On their heroes return, Rogers was awarded several swords of honour, £200 plus, and promoted to Commander, with commensurate financial rewards and 'smart' money being awarded to his crew.

Rogers was also given command of the brand new packet, **Countess of Chichester**, which he commanded successfully for many years, before transferring to the Holyhead Packet station. There, after having devoted most of his working life to the PO packet service, William Rogers died in January 1825, a relatively young man of 47, completely worn out by the rigours of the service.

While the packet commanders enjoyed considerable social status around Falmouth, their basic pay was modest enough, standing at £78 per annum from the 1760s up until 1790, irrespective of whether Britain was at peace or at war. The wartime rate was only raised to £104 per annum in 1791, or £8 per lunar month. With new packets costing from £4,000 to £6,000, most of the owner/commanders' accumulated wealth came out of their profits on carrying freight and passengers – of which more later.

At the end of their service most established commanders enjoyed a grace and favour pension, loosely based on the number of years' service, but usually amounting to £100 or £150 per annum. Their widows were not automatically catered for, but some received sums in the order of £60 per annum, especially during wartime, or following death in service.

*John Bull's Silver Pig
The celebrated toothpick holder, which was reputedly seized by the Falmouth customs officers and later bought back by him at a knock-down price. Now one of the prized exhibits of the National Maritime Museum Cornwall, it is on display in the Packet Gallery*

6 Packet Crews

Lisbon *Muleta* 1800

At its height the Falmouth packet service employed over 1,200 seamen. Prior to 1783, the manning levels on the various packets differed considerably from route to route, and in peacetime ranged from eighteen men on the North American packets, to twenty-six on the Lisbon route. During 1783 the peacetime compliment of the Lisbon packets was increased to 30, by the addition of a surgeon, first mate, and two seamen. But the numbers were again reduced in 1791, on the adoption of the new standard packets, each with the same number of hands.

In wartime the packet crews were increased to man the extra guns carried. Prior to 1791, they were raised to a notional 60 men each – though only 59 were actually carried. The wages of the phantom seamen being kept as a perk by the packet agent. Allowing one phantom seaman missing from each of the eighteen packets in commission, this perk was worth at least £230 per annum at the ordinary seaman's wage of £13, and much more if allowed at the able seaman's rate of pay. Later the Post Office capitalised on this former practice, and diverted the phantom's wages to the *sick and hurt fund*.

On the introduction of the new style packets, in the early 1790s (which carried only six broadside guns – three a side), the established wartime compliment was cut to 30 men per packet. Doing away with the need for a second mate, three petty officers and 26 seamen. At the same time the established peacetime compliments were reduced – from 30 to 21 – with the loss of nine seamen's jobs on each packet (see Compliments and Wages pp123–4).

Packet Crews and their Normal Duties

The masters, or sailing masters – undertook the day to day navigation of the packets, and to a large extent advised their commanders on ship handling – especially in those instances where there was *a gentleman commander*. Nat Uring, who sailed as master on the West India packet **Prince**, (1) in 1703–4, was particularly unimpressed with his captain. When attacked by a privateer, *The Captain left me to do as I thought best* … After the action *Our Captain was now come to Life again ... we narrowly escaped running upon the Bishops and Clarks,* … some of the Western Rocks of Scilly.

In the peacetime Lisbon service no mates were carried until after 1783, and the master kept regular deck watches along with the commander. But, on the long haul packets the commander did not keep regular watches, and up until 1791 they carried two mates and a master. These three officers worked an irregular rolling three-watch system – enjoying a comfortable one watch on, and two watches off.

Each having alternate charge of *the other watch* whenever he *held the deck*. It did not benefit the hands in any way, they were still divided into two watches – starboard, and larboard – keeping watch and watch about.

Masters – regularly took command of a packet in their commander's absence, and some attained a command of their own in time. From pre-1760 to 1783 masters were paid £26 per annum in peacetime, and £39 in time of war. After 1783 the corresponding pay rates stood at £39 and £52 per annum respectively. Towards the end of the Napoleonic Wars their pay had been increased to £5 per lunar month – £65 per annum. But, with the return of peace in 1815, pay was quickly reduced to the established peacetime rate. In the masters' case to £39 per annum, or £3 per lunar month. In 1818 representations were made by the commanders that this was no longer adequate, and that for some time they had been obliged to pay above the *established* rates to keep their crews. The PMG agreed with their arguments, but rather than increase the established rates, they authorised a lump sum of £210 per annum as aid, to enable the commanders to continue to pay the rates allowed at the end of the war. The pay of the other ranks was reviewed and revised at the same time as that of the masters.

Mates – when appointed, were deck officers keeping full watches. At such times they were in full control of the ship, being responsible to the commander for her safe handling, and the behaviour and discipline of their part of the crew. However, when working the three-watch system described above, some of the normal bonding between watch officers and *their part* of the crew must have been lost. First mates lived aft (or rather just aft of amidships) having a small match-wood cabin in the 'tween-decks, between the crew and the passengers.

Second mates – were in an invidious position, being little more than glorified bosuns. Having no cabin they lived with the crew, sleeping in hammocks. However, they kept deck watches, and ate with the master, surgeon and mate, in the mess-room.

Surgeons – were very important members of the crew, especially in these small vessels where a large number of men were crowded into a confined space. Their regular duties were light enough, but at times they were sorely pressed. That a number of them are known by name lies chiefly in the fact that so many died on passage, usually of yellow fever. The level of qualification required for a packet surgeon is not known, and on board some packets the surgeon was given the task of sorting and recording the receipt and delivery of the mails at intermediate ports of call. Like the mates they had a small cabin, located between the crew and the passengers. Under Royal Naval control, after 1823, there was a panel of unattached surgeons, who were appointed to packets in rotation as and when required.

Petty officers – in the main self-explanatory, their duties

conformed with normal merchant shipping practice. The boatswain, or bosun, answered to the mate for the working of the ship, its rigging, and the behaviour of the crew. The carpenter was responsible for the maintenance of the hull, boats and spars, effecting all running repairs during a voyage. Similarly, the sailmaker was responsible for the maintenance and repair of the sails, together with making any new replacements required on voyage. A gunner, only carried in wartime, was responsible for maintaining the carriage guns and small arms, along with ensuring the safe, dry, stowage of the gunpowder and shot. Usually mature, ex-naval gunners, whenever a packet went into action they were normally in charge of the long, stern-chase, guns, upon which the safety of the packets so often depended when trying to disable an overtaking enemy. The petty officers all lived and messed in the main deck, usually slinging their hammocks outside their respective store rooms.

Packetmen – were much like any other British tar, and consisted of a fair mix of experienced sailors, aspiring young landsmen, and idle hands. And, despite regulations to the contrary, contained a fair number of foreign seamen. Some authorities speak of them being picked men, prime seamen all, while others refer to them as *lead swingers, the dregs of the sea,* or the *scum of the maritime backwaters* – but 'packet rats' were a later American phenomena. As with any such amorphous group, all such descriptions applied in some measure.

While there is insufficient room to fully describe their duties here, it is sufficient to say that whatever had to be done, a seaman did! Their basic abilities to *hand, reef and steer,* were foregone assumptions. But in addition each had to stand his turn of watches and lookout; take soundings; man the boats in all weathers, and a host of other shipboard tasks. More arduous work came in the form of working the windlass to haul the anchors; or the remorseless pumping in bad weather, as the ship worked her seams in a heavy seaway while *shipping 'em green* on deck. With only one or two token ordinary seamen carried on most packets, no job was too menial for an able seamen, whether it was slushing down the masts, overhauling the rigging, holystoning the decks, polishing the bright-work, or scrubbing off the ordure under the ship's heads – all were a daily part of a seaman's lot.

Manning and the Impress Service

At times the service was beset by manning problems, but the regular nature of the work usually attracted mature seamen, family men looking for service stability. This all changed in time of war, when the service was constantly under pressure, with extra routes being introduced, frequent losses, and extra packets being brought into commission. Basing a unit of the impress service at Falmouth had a marked effect on the availability of casual seamen. Almost anything was preferable to being pressed, and for the packetmen there was some insurance against enforced naval service in the form of *press protections* – though these were often ignored.

As Capt Slade, the officer commanding the impress service at Falmouth, noted some time after the 1810 Packet Mutiny–

> ... *it is my humble Opinion the Packet Seamen would soon return to their former state of insubordination, if the activity of the Impress is checked ... in a Port where there are Eleven Hundred Seamen in the employ of Government, without Martial Law to keep them in order.*

At the time he was defending his job, and he *was very jealous about the number of packet seamen protected by me.* – Saverland the packet agent.

To prevent a total collapse of British mercantile marine in wartime, press protections were issued to key sectors of British merchant shipping. Normally issued by British customs house officers – under authority from the Admiralty – the packet agent was specially deputed to issue those for the Falmouth Packet Service.

On the outbreak of each foreign conflict, the crews of the PO packets were among the first to enjoy press protection. Whenever they were paid off, seamen were fair game for the press gangs, and for convenience a form of continuous service was adopted by the packet commanders at Falmouth. Instead of paying off at the end of each voyage, their crews were kept on the books (for victualling if not actually on full pay). During their stay at Falmouth they worked the ship as required, as well as enjoying short spells of shore leave. But, as the agent wrote in 1813:

> Our seamen do not like to remain long on shore. If the packet be a month under repair, the men are always anxious to go to sea in another packet. There must always, however, be from twenty to sixty seamen without ships. These must be protected and our number being about 1,200 seamen there cannot be less.

Saverland was bending the rules, hence Slade's jealousy.

One event that could break this chain of protected employment was the loss of a packet – either by wreck or enemy action. By long merchant tradition, as soon as a ship was lost, the pay of her crew ceased and their press protections immediately became null and void!

After the packet **Duke of Cumberland**, was wrecked near St Augustine, North America, in September 1776, the merchant vessel **Betsey** was hired to bring home her crew, the mails and dispatches. On the **Betsey**'s arrival at Spithead she was boarded and the packetmen were swiftly 'pressed' into HM Ships **Coureageux**, and **Royal Oak**. The men duly petitioned the PMG for their release, in order to return to the packet service.

There were many similar instances, and on this occasion the

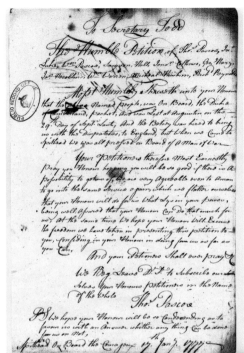

men were lucky, as the Admiralty was prepared to comply with the PMG's request, and they were soon returned to Falmouth.

The fear of impressment was a constant one. While the packet **Thynne** was being overhauled on the Thames during 1782, Samuel Kelly was:

> ... sent to Trinity House to get a lighter for our ballast, and supposing my protection (to keep me from the press) had expired, I obtained a new one, when having reached Trinity House I discovered by the date of the order given me, that my old protection was good for that day, and that my new one did not commence till the day following, this put me in a fright as my old protection was not with me, but I got on board safe without being over hauled by the press gangs.

The threat of the press gangs, and the reassuring comfort of a press protection, were material factors in sustaining the wartime manning levels of the packet service. Once the impress service was withdrawn from Falmouth desertions increased significantly, as Saverland reported in June 1814:

> The **Fox** Packet for Surinam sailed early this morning four men short of her Compliment. Captain Tilly is by no means to be blamed on Account of the delay, having completed his compliment several times over but has not been able to keep them on board, the Impress being done away, by the Gang having been paid off by order of the Admiralty.

Discipline Afloat

Contrary to popular belief the packet service did not come under naval discipline, until the Admiralty took control in 1823, and then only for those serving on the naval packets. As early as 1704/5 Dummer had requested the right to impress seamen for the service, but this was never approved. There are no known cases of flogging in the packet service, though the petty officers may well have used starters to move the seamen quickly about their duties.

For the seamen the only significant punishment was dismissal and consequential the loss of their *press protection*. Minor offences may have been covered by a system of shipboard fines, but if so these were not formally codified. Control of offending seamen was by means of a *Black Book*, kept by the packet agent. In 1782, Stephen Bell distributed a fresh set of RULES *to be observed by the Captains, Officers, and Seamen, belonging to his Majesty's Pacquet-Boats on the* FALMOUTH *Station*. Like the naval *Articles of War*, these were read aloud to the crew at each packet muster (see Instructions ...p125).

Offenders and supplicants appeared before a committee of captains, consisting of at least three packet captains and chaired by the packet agent. Commanders were also required to appear before these committees of their peers to answer for any alleged misconduct, including the loss of their packets, and/or the mails.

However, in July 1814, after finding:

> ... *that Captain Richards ought to have kept his Vessel more before the Wind, to have enabled him to have used his brass guns out of the stern ports &c. &c. &c. and that their Lordships direct that Captain Richards shall not be again suffered to command any Vessel in their Lordships Service,...*

The committee had gone too far in presuming to pass sentence and instruct their Lordships. And it was realised (with some embarrassment) that there was no legal constitution for such courts. As Saverland later contritely acknowledged:

> ... *that their Lordships do not approve the further proceedings of the Court in passing sentence, and carrying that sentence into execution; upon which I beg to observe that having no instructions to guide us in these Enquiries, we have been led to adopt the custom of Naval Courts Martial and to pass sentence upon Officers brought before us, which has been almost the invariable practice upon this station, as the numerous reports will shew. At the same time I beg to state, that I perfectly agree with you that the practice has been wrong; and I am of opinion that future Courts will feel much relieved from a responsibility, assumed, which does not belong to them.*

> I am Sir &c. Christopher Saverland

Thereafter they were only to report and recommend.

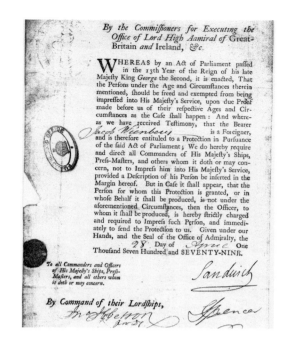

Sick and Hurt

At first there was no form of pension for the packetmen, but by 1703 a relief fund had been established for those hurt in action. Funded by deductions of 10d. per man per month, this fund was held and distributed at the discretion of the Packet Agent at Falmouth – a practice which (as we have seen) was open to abuse. By the 1760s a charge of one shilling per man per month was allowed by the PO, for the relief of distressed seamen. Just who held this fund or how it was administered is not known, but perhaps it still lay with the packet agent at Falmouth. After the reforms of the early 1790s the PO provided for this fund by redirecting the phantom seamen's wages (as mentioned earlier in this chapter). How this later fund was administered is not clear, and there appears to have been no automatic right to pensions as such, though very early on there were prescribed rates of compensation for loss of limbs during hostilities.

In the 1690s annual *Smart Payments* were set at:

For each Arm of Leg amputated above the elbow or knee	£8
For each Arm or Leg amputated below the elbow or knee	£6 13s 4d
For the loss of one Eye	£4
For the loss of both Eyes	£12
If the pupils of both Eyes were lost	£14

An augmented scale, in force during the Napoleonic Wars, is illustrated by an incident involving the packet **Duke of Marlborough** (2). Approaching Barbados on March 27th 1807, she was attacked by a heavily manned schooner privateer, of 14 guns. After a night long running engagement, the attacker withdrew having sustained heavy casualties, but she in her turn had taken a toll of the packet's crew. On their return to England, Francis Freeling advised the PMG:

> It has always been usual in cases of this sort to apply to the Lords of the Treasury for permission to reward the parties for their bravery and good conduct. In this instance it has saved the Revenue £4,000 which must have been paid had the Packet been captured by the Enemy.
>
> ... and apply to the Treasury for permission to allow four Months pay and Smart money to the Officers and Crew ... the pay amounts to £228. 8s., the Smart money to £45. 15s., making together £274. 3s.

On this occasion the casualties (or their dependants) awarded smart money were:

William James	Act. commander wounded in the foot	£10 10s
John McKinnon	Master wounded in the face	£5 5s
James Price	(Mate) musket ball in the arm	£5 0s
Thomas Soloman,	Able Seaman killed	£10 0s
Robert Clemence	Able Seaman shattered thigh (hopeless)	£10 0s
John Gilbert	Able Seamen splinter in the arm	£5 0s

While the compensation for the more common injuries was covered by these scales, the packet agent occasionally made a higher recommendation. The injuries received by James Elliot so moved the agent, though the higher payment recommended to Francis Freeling was unprecedented:

20 June 1814

Sir,

I am favoured with your Letter of the 17th instant respecting the case of James Elliot, who lost his Hands & part of both Arms, below the Elbow joint, by a Cannon shot in the very severe Action between His Majesty's Packet **Duke of Marlborough**, Captain John Bull and the **Primrose** Sloop of War, whom I recommended for a Pension of £30 a-Year. There is no precedent on record, for granting so large a sum to a Packet Seaman disabled in Action, neither has a Seaman before survived so great a calamity. The present object is nearly well of his Wounds, and walking about the Streets, but unable to dress, or feed himself. If he had lost only one hand, he might have turned a Wheel, rowed in a Boat, or done some little thing towards his support; his situation is greatly commiserated, & I trust & hope the sum I have recommended, will not be thought too much for a gallant Packet Seaman, in such deplorable circumstances.

I am Sir &c. Christopher Saverland.

Throughout the packet era there were many deserving cases, which received no financial help as there was no automatic right to a pension for lesser employees. So, while the PO supported a great number of *pensioners of state*, in the event of incapacitating injury received during the normal course of employment, or age infirmity, the seamen had to first petition the PMG for relief. Thus, while in 1781, the Dukes of Marlborough, and Grafton, and the heirs of the Duke of Schomberg, were drawing handsome annual pensions of £5,000, £4,700 and £4,000 respectively from the PO revenues; packet commander's widows were receiving from £30 to £60 per annum, and the poor packetman and his dependant relatives had to be content with a mere £3, £5 or £10 a year, if they were lucky.

Bermuda Sloop 1807

7 Life on Board

The Seamen

While living conditions for all on board the packets were damp, cramped and uncomfortable, for the seamen they were very basic and totally devoid of any comfort. Fortunately most foremast-hands knew little better ashore or afloat.

Schooner 1815

In these vessels, measuring little more than 80 feet by 23 feet overall, space was always at a premium. The crew's quarters, especially when carrying their pre 1790s wartime compliment of 60 hands, were desperately crowded. All accommodation was housed between decks (that is on the main deck and under the weather deck). Here there was scarcely ever more five feet clear headroom, under the deck beams, and prior to 1790 there was insufficient room for all hands to simultaneously sling a hammock. Many had to share watch and watch about, and other less fortunate individuals – the boys – slept wherever they could.

Even after the early 1790s, when the wartime compliments were reduced to 28 men, conditions remained cramped, though there was marginally more space per individual than on board a contemporary man-of-war. The seamen occupied most of the forward part of the standard packets, but they shared this space with the ship's caboose, or galley, which was located right in the eyes of the ship, and the boatswain's and the carpenter's stores, which lay on either side of the galley. These two petty officers probably berthed and messed just outside the doorways to their stores, along with the sailmaker and gunner. The galley stores were kept in the forepeak, below the caboose, while the gunner's magazine was sited aft in the most secure part of the vessel, on the orlop under the cabins

The remaining 22 crew members occupied a space of about 30 feet long by 23 feet wide, but large parts of this were obstructed by hatchways, gangways, deck stanchions, parts of the officers' cabins, the pump barrels and the fore-mast trunk. Four seamen usually comprised a mess, sharing the daily chores of eating and living. There was no provision for personal privacy, though each hand was allowed his sea chest, which also served as a seat. Their chests, once as large as a seaman could physically handle, were restricted to 36 inches long by 14 inches wide and deep, by the end of the 1780s. Left unlocked by the custom of the sea, the contents of a seaman's chest were sacrosanct and any breech of this trust was a major social crime on shipboard.

When on an even keel, the main deck lay just inches above the water line, at sea the lee side was many feet under, and the crew's accommodation was a dark, dank, foetid hole. There were no portholes, skylights, deck-lights or ventilators. Some light and air filtered through the hatches when open, but when battened down in foul weather there was no provision for natural light or ventilation. The use of artificial light was restricted because of both cost, and the risk of fire.

There were, of course, no toilet facilities for the ordinary hands, beyond the 'bucket and chuck-it' variety for the less agile, or a precarious perch on an alternately soaring and plunging beak head for the able-bodied. Here, with one's nether regions dangling in space and hanging on for grim death, there was a very real likelihood of being drenched by flying spray, if not completely engulfed by a surging sea.

In most packets the caboose containing the galley-stove was located in the 'tween-decks, forward of the foremast trunk. Here cooking conditions were appalling, and a more unsuitable place would be hard to find. Packets were lively craft, and in the bows the incessant plunging and soaring motion was amplified. Gallons of boiling liquid, sluicing about in large copper cauldrons, threatened a scalding, if not lethal, shower to any unwary cook. In bad weather, the galley fires were frequently extinguished, and all hands put on cold tack. Fire being one of the greatest hazards on wooden ships – the galley-stove was usually set on a brick platform. However, in one of the packets in which Samuel Kelly served (possibly the Spanish-built **Grenville** (2)), only a sheet of lead protected the deck below from the heat of the galley-stove. On one voyage they found that:

> … by some carelessness, the lead beneath the fire-place covering the deck, was melted, and the fire burnt through the deck, but providentially the carpenter, going to his storeroom in the cockpit, discovered the fire overhead, and it was soon extinguished. Had it not been discovered so early,… the consequences might have been fatal, and our loss never accounted for.

Everyone's food was prepared in communal copper-boilers, whose cleanliness often left much to be desired.

> On one passage many of the crew were attacked with excruciating pains in their bowels, and I believe nearly half of our men were confined to their hammocks. This disease our surgeon supposed to be the effect of poison. Accordingly the copper boilers were examined, and a quantity of verdigris was discovered on the inside of the pease copper, which the cook's mate had neglected to clean, as usual. For my part, I escaped by not liking the pease soup, …. (Samuel Kelly, 1781)

The diet was generally ample but monotonous. Each commander was allowed a daily sum per man for the purchase of victuals. Based on the bulk cost of staple foods, this sum was occasionally reviewed against prevailing London prices, but there was no automatic adjustment for inflation – though a slightly higher sum was allowed in wartime.

In the 1760s the commanders were allowed $7\frac{1}{2}$d (just over 3p) per day per man, or 4s 4¹/₂d (22p) per week. Increased by 1781 to 9d (nearly 4p) per day, this increase came into effect while Kelly was serving in the packets. Even so, his opinion of the rations served was not complimentary:

> This ship being a contract one, our provisions were of infamous quality, the beef appeared coarse, and such as is cured for Negroes, the barrels of pork consisted of pigs' heads with iron rings in the nose, pigs' feet and pigs' tails with much hair thereon. Each man had six pounds of bread and five pounds of salted meat per week, but neither beer, spirits nor candles were allowed.

The provisions provided on a contract packet were probably no worse than those served on the PO owned vessels. New calculations made during Lord Walsingham's time as PMG allowed a little more bread and salt-meat, and a generous amount of beer – one gallon per day. But, the fresh water carried was barely palatable and the diet was still monotonous.

During the 1790s the wartime victualling allowance was raised to 1s (5p) per day, where it officially remained for over twenty years. By 1812 the effects of wartime inflation compelled the commanders at Falmouth to write to the PMG pointing out that there was a:

> ...bona fide loss to the Captain of every Packet in your Lordships' service of nearly three hundred pounds p-annum by victualling the seamen only, independent of some other grievances which we labour under ...

They drew attention to the current victualling rates for other Public Boards - the Board of Excise allowing 1s 11d (nearly 10p), and the Customs 1s 6d (7.5p), ... and 18d P-month P-man for Fire & Candles. They took the further liberty of enclosing ... a true and faithful statement of the present prices of provisions, to enable their Lordships... to form a correct judgement on this subject. (see victualling p126)

While the scale of provisions quoted differed slightly from the above list, the increase in costs was significant. Salt beef and pork stood at 7¹/₂d per pound, as against 3d and a gallon of peas cost 2s against 3d in the 1790s. Even though the bread allowance had been reduced from 7 to 4 pounds per week, and there was now no mention of beer or oatmeal in the account, the actual cost of victualling one man for a week stood at 9s10d or 1s5d per day. In the face of irrefutable evidence the PMG reluctantly authorised some additional aid to the commanders.

In addition to the basic provisions allowed as above, there was an occasional rum issue. Unlike the RN, this was not a general issue, but a special allowance introduced when the North American route was changed to include calls at Halifax throughout the winter. The ration was half a pint of spirits mixed with water issued in such a manner as the commanders think proper. The 60 gallons carried was to be used frugally, but the stock could be replenished at Halifax. In addition each man was issued with a greatcoat, costing 28 shillings, to enable him to 'stand the deck' in the inclement climate.

Officers' Accommodation

The officers' cabins, such as they were, lay towards the stern, as did the commander's quarters and the passenger accommodation. Here, though they ate much the same food as the hands, living was a little easier.

In some earlier packets the officers' cabins formed a physical barrier between the crew and the commander, but in the 1790s standard packets a range of these cabins ran fore and aft on either side. Small matchwood partitioned structures, these gave an illusion of privacy to the master, mate and surgeon. These cabins encroached on the crew's space, opening directly onto their mess deck. As befitted their senior status, those of the master and surgeon were slightly larger than the mate's, being about six feet square, as against six feet by four feet. Abaft of the surgeon's cabin lay an irregular shaped pantry, which opened aft into the day cabin. Here the steward looked after the cabin stores for the passengers, preparing such delicacies as the galley would otherwise have ruined. The doorway to the pantry was formed in a timber bulkhead, running across the vessel just forward of the mainmast trunk, which now partitioned the hands from the captain and passengers. Abaft of this bulkhead lay the central day cabin or mess room, down either side of which the run of matchwood cabins continued. Here they formed six passenger cabins – twin berth, six feet by four feet six, hutches – three on either side of the vessel. The central mess room was eighteen feet long tapering, as the hull of the packet narrowed towards the stern, from thirteen feet to ten. In action this space doubled as the surgeon's operating theatre and sick bay. Its only concessions to comfort being a large table with two bench seats, a small skylight overhead, and a stove near the forward bulkhead.

A central doorway in the after bulkhead of the mess room gave access to a quarter-turning companionway to the upper deck, behind which was encased the trunk of the mizzen mast. To starboard lay a doorway to the captain's stateroom if such a term could be applied to a six foot by eight foot irregular shaped compartment. Another doorway to port linked the mess room with the stern cabin, or saloon, via a short passageway.

This saloon, nominally the captain's day cabin, was usually commandeered by the 'great and the good', as their day and night cabin for the duration of a voyage. Extending across the full width of the stern, with plush banquet seating, the saloon enjoyed the luxury of daylight (and occasionally fresh air), from a couple of stern windows and an overhead skylight, together with the warmth from another small

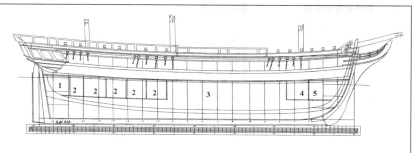

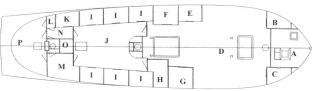

New Standard Packet, c.1790

Dimensions

Length	80ft
Breadth	23 ft
Depth of Hold	10 ft
Height (Between decks)	6 ft
Tonnage (Builders Measure)	180 tons

Legend

Compartments on the Main Deck (Between decks) –

A.	Galley	B	Boatswain's Store
C.	Carpenter's Store	D.	Crew's living space
E.	Mate's cabin	F.	Master's cabin
G.	Surgeon's cabin	H.	Pantry
I.	Passengers' cabins	J.	Passengers' mess room and day cabin
K.	Passengers' dressing room		
L.	Water closet	M.	Captain's Stateroom
N.	Passage way	O.	Half Turning stairway to the weather deck
P.	Saloon		

Compartments beneath the Main deck

1. Lazarette – specie and valuables
2. Dry Store-rooms on the Orlop (including a bread-room, mail-room, and the magazine)
3. Hold – largely occupied by water casks
4. Sailmaker's store
5. Forepeak – galley stores

stove. Just forward of the saloon, adjoining on the port quarter, was a water closet. This had both direct access from the saloon, and from the passageway between the saloon and the mess-room – leaving two doors to bolt! This short corridor also gave access to a small dressing room alongside the water closet. Apart from the amenities mentioned there were few other material comforts.

Disease & Quarantine

Apart from the dangers of fire and the normal 'hazards of the sea', the packetmen's worst dread was disease. In the Mediterranean plague was the constant fear, but far more common were outbreaks of cholera, and typhus. Frequently reaching as far north as Lisbon during the summer months, these epidemics raged until the cooler autumn weather reduced their virulence. Plague was often rampant throughout the Mediterranean. During the summer and autumn of 1813, there was a major outbreak at Malta, and lesser ones at Gibraltar, and Cadiz. At this time quarantining ships arriving from 'fever ports' was the only known preventative and the packets were no exception. Between July and December 1813 no less than nine Mediterranean packets, and one from Cadiz and Corunna, were sent to Stangate Creek (a remote marshy creek on the Blackwater, near the mouth of the Thames), to perform quarantine. Apart from the additional week or so that it took get to and from Stangate, each packet's crew and passengers were detained in idleness for two to three weeks. In 1813 such forced detention placed an exceptional strain on the service, at a time of heavy war losses. Fortunately their enforced detention was the only price paid, there being no reported cases of active disease on board the packets at Stangate, and no recorded deaths.

On the West India station it was often a very different story. Here yellow fever and malaria were endemic, and while the beneficial effects of the cinchona bark were appreciated, if not fully understood in connection with the latter, yellow fever had no known cure.

Yellow fever was the scourge of the Caribbean, and most ships calling there suffered to some degree. The very nature of the service, with monthly packets calling at several islands in succession, left their crews highly exposed. Few fever seasons passed without some packetmen becoming victims, and passengers were equally at risk, many of them dying on route to Britain:

> Falmouth, Oct. 31st, 1793 – On Tuesday arrived the **Boyd** packet from Jamaica. There was a very great sickness on board her, which raged so furiously, that the Captain, two passengers, and twelve seamen, died on their passage.

The thought of a virulent disease being rapidly transmitted by contagious mail bags, through the main sorting office at London, and on to the offices of central Government and international merchants across the capital, caused Samuel Pellew, Collector of Customs at Falmouth, and others great anxiety. While condemned by many as alarmist, Pellew's staff were responsible for enforcing the current legislation. He was fully aware of its inadequacy, and was very concerned to see a wholesale reform of the quarantine laws, and the introduction of a strict but practical quarantine process.

The existing quarantine procedures applied equally to packets as to other shipping, but there was the potentially fatal flaw in that for reasons of expediency the mails were permitted to be landed on arrival. To prevent the spread of any infection the folded letters were cut through in several places, fumigated, and soaked in vinegar. Just how effective this practice was is very uncertain. It certainly rendered the addresses and contents of many letters almost indecipherable.

Just how easily disease might have been introduced into Britain is shown by the following events involving the **Montagu**. Over running her homeport in heavy weather, Capt Watkins ran his packet into Dartmouth Haven on February 15th 1817, where she remained over two weeks before returning to Falmouth on March 2nd. The local newspapers made no mention of fever or loss of life on this voyage, but a customs' report revealed that:

> Five of her crew had died of yellow fever during the voyage, and eighteen others were down with the same complaint. The Captain did not hoist the quarantine flag at Dartmouth, as he should have done, and, strange to tell, the Customs did not visit the vessel there, as they were supposed to do. But quite a number of Dartmouth people went aboard, and some of the ship's company, including the doctor and one of the sick men went ashore. When the vessel reached Falmouth the master, on being questioned in the usual way by the Customs as to health of company during the voyage, made many misleading statements. The ship's papers were forwarded to the Privy Council by the officers, there being doubt as to the master's bona–fides, and when it was discovered later that there was yellow fever on board it was too late to recall the papers for fumigation.

It is not certain what the doubts were as to Capt John Watkins' bona fides, but his behaviour warranted severe censure. However, he was a war hero, and retained command of the **Montagu** until she was paid off in 1825, and then went on to command HM Packet **Sylph** as a civilian commander, until his death in June 1828.

The loss of life on the temporary packet **Boyd** has already been noted, and there were many other similar tragedies. When the **Penelope** arrived at Falmouth from Jamaica on Wednesday December 2nd 1801, she reported the loss of ten seamen from yellow fever, along with Mr. Nicholls, surgeon of the packet, and only son of Mr. Michael Nicholls, Marazion, an amiable young man, and highly esteemed. Such reports were extremely distressing. In the close-knit community of Falmouth, one or more of the deceased would have been personally known to most people, and such reports were a constant reminder of just another of the hazards faced by their seamen every day. Again in 1809:

> On Tuesday (19/9/1809), *the* **Princess Augusta** *packet, arrived from the Windward Islands, having lost her Capt, St. Aubyn, Mr. Melhuish mate, and ten seamen with the yellow fever. Her whole crew consisted of but 32 men and boys. This we believe, is a greater proportion of deaths than any packets crew have experienced from this dreadful disease, – and is the more extraordinary, as the packet was not down so far as Jamaica. The last man died sixteen days before she arrived at Falmouth. The fever disappeared, as the ship increased her northern latitude; but she is still under quarantine.*

While the losses were not as heavy as on the **Boyd** fifteen years previously, they were just as shocking. A trawl of similar accounts reveals that whereas over 92 men were killed in action on board the packets (between 1740 and 1815), at least 99 died of yellow fever (between 1780 and 1828), and eight of these were surgeons. Now eight may not sound very many, but it represented a significantly high degree of risk in attending the afflicted.

Heavy loss of life due to disease was also experienced on the Brazil run, though never of the same magnitude as on the West India packets. Yellow fever continued to take its toll right up until the end of the packet era. In 1850 a number of alarming reports emanated from Rio.

> May 24th – H.M. packet **Penguin**, ... *arrived on Sunday morning, from Rio ... Three of her (steerage) passengers, Messrs. Cobling, Shaen, and J. Like, died on board of yellow fever; also the steward's mate, Clemow; and the sail maker, Meek.*
>
> May 31st – H. M. packet **Express**, ... *from Rio ... (where) Yellow fever ... was still raging violently; it was computed that at least 12,000 persons had died ... Several vessels lying there had lost two-thirds of their crews.*
>
> July 12th – ... *the* **Crane**, *Lieut. Parsons, arrived from Rio Janeiro ... We regret to state that Mr. Ball, the assistant-surgeon of this packet, died May 19th, five days after leaving Rio.*

To the very last the surgeons and their assistants remained the most at risk.

8 Packets at War 1690–1783

The formation of the Falmouth Packet Service was a direct consequence of war with France, and for virtually half of the eighteenth century Britain was embroiled in one war or another, with France, Spain, Holland and Anglo-America featuring as our main protagonists at different times. Each war placed new demands on the packet service, and at its close there were invariably attempts to rationalise and economise.

Packet brig 1816

How to effectively protect the mails was a constant mind teaser. While the security of the mails and dispatches was paramount, economic constraints had to be considered. Exclusive Royal Navy convoy was out of the question. It was far too expensive and there weren't enough warships to go round. If there had been, they would have carried the mails and despatches, obviating any need for a packet service. Sailing in a merchant convoy was not a viable option. Speed was of the essence and convoys were notoriously slow. On a few occasions packets were offered individual safe convoy by the RN, but only for short distances through enemy infested waters.

The initial view was that packets should be of sufficient size and force to be able to fight off any opportunist attacks by small privateers – say of 14 to 20 guns. This level of armament entailed high operating costs, which the Treasury found unacceptable. All hinged on the number and size of carriage guns carried, which in turn dictated the minimum size of vessel that could carry those guns, and the minimum number of men required to work them in action.

The precise size and armament of the first packets is not known, but at Falmouth there was a marked preference for the two older packets in the early 1700s. The **Allyance**, and **Expedition**, were each considered *a Ship of Force, therefore not so liable to the Insults of an Enemy*. The **Expedition** carrying 26 guns and a crew of 90, was a potentially significant opponent, but nevertheless she was taken by French privateers in March 1708.

The first packets did not carry 'letters of marque,' which caused problems in the 1690s when they took several lightly armed merchant traders as prizes. They were initially condemned to the Crown as 'Droits of Admiralty', and sold. Petitions were submitted, and in January and February 1697(8), royal warrants granted one-third of the proceeds to the packet commanders and seamen; one-third to the Receiver General of the PO revenue; while retaining one-third as droits. Taken by the packets **Allyance** and **Expedition**, the prizes concerned, included the:

St. John, of Bordeaux, laden with salt fish

St. John Bonadventure, laden with sugar

St. Joseph, carrying wool and hides

La Nostre Dame La Aimanaide, Algiers to Lisbon with barilia and soap

Margaret, of Nantes, Lisbon for Arcassone, with pitch and bread,
St. *Francis Dearis*, a small English-built sloop from Hispaniola, with sugar, hides, tobacco, and indigo.

The question of letters of marque was addressed in Dummer's *Terms for settling a monthly intelligence between England and the Island Plantations in the West Indies*, dated June 18th 1702. But, while they may have been issued with a letter of marque, Dummer's standing orders instructed his commanders ... *to make straight for their destination in the West Indies (Barbadoes); to avoid all contact with other ships; to avoid use of the guns unless forced to do so...* A policy that was later applied to all PO packets.

Some commanders disobeyed their instructions. When the **Bridgeman** took the Danish galliot **Crown *and Wine Cask*** in July 1703, there was little that Dummer could do to discipline her commander – he and his packet being taken by the enemy just three days later. However, when the **Mansbridge** arrived at Falmouth in the following month, just after capturing a French vessel from Newfoundland, her commander was dismissed!

The first vessels on the West Indies being inadequate, they were soon replaced by five 200 ton packets. These were two decked vessels armed with 20 carriage guns, carrying 24 sweeps for rowing them in calms – a last resort in dire emergencies. But even this level of armament was not proof against capture.

When returning to England in the latter part of 1707, Nathaniel Uring's **Prince George**, was chased by two French privateers. During a chase of over four hours, he caused the *great Part of the Seamen's Chests to be hove over-board, beginning with my own*, in order to lighten the ship. These were quickly followed by:

> ... *our Boat, all our spare Masts and Yards, and what other lumber was upon Deck; the Anchors were cut away from the Bows, and several Cables cut in Pieces and tossed over-board; we also threw over-board several Barrels of Indigo and other Goods...*

But it was not enough –

> ... *on Opening our Ports the Water came into the Ship in such Quantities, that it washed clear over the Guns, and wet the Priming; and not only so, but filled the Deck with Water, which render'd it impossible to fight our Guns between decks.*

Fearing treachery, Uring had previously caused his

> *Ensign to be nailed to the Staff, ... that none of my People should be able to strike it; and having all I was worth on Board, was not willing to lose it easily, being resolved not to surrender until there was no possibility of keeping her.*

For a while they kept the enemy at bay with musketry fire through their loopholes. However, after a close action lasting *five glasses* – two and a half hours – and:

> *Seeing my People would not help me, and the Privateer ready for boarding,*

I *went down into the Cabbin to heave over-board the Mail, that it might not fall into the Hands of the Enemy, of which I had particular Charge ... while I was putting the Mail out of the Cabbin Port, my Lieutenant John Bourn, ... gave up the Ship; and the French were down between Decks before I had thrown the Mail over-board, so I was obliged to barracade the Cabbin Door till I had done so...*

To be fair to the seamen, their packet was not well designed for fighting. Open railings around the quarterdeck left the crew dreadfully exposed when forced to steer on deck – as an iron tiller mounted in the cabin *would not command her.*

... the Privateer's *Men ... fired furiously upon the Quarter-Deck, and wounded the Man at the Helm, of which he afterwards died. ...*

Every Creature we had upon Deck was kill'd by the Enemy's Small Shot, and every man that staid there any Time was either kill'd or wounded, except myself, who came off safe.

Their main adversary, the **Fortune**, carried 26 guns and 200 men. Her consort was of similar size but played little part in the action. The **Prince George** was taken to St. Malo, and Uring remained a *Prisoner in France Nine Months*, before he obtained *leave to go to England on my Parole of Honour, in order to procure an equal Exchange in my Room, or to return to France in Three Months.* An exchange was arranged, but according to Dummer's later reports, at least nine of his packets were lost between 1702 and 1709 – most of them to the enemy.

Again little is known of the armament of the packets during either the War of the Austrian Succession, or the Seven Years War. However, during 1741 it was noted at Falmouth, that *Captain Lovell is come down with his new Ship, or rather old one Cutt in two and lengthened to carry 20 Guns great and small;* and in 1744 ... *'tis thought ye Captains of ye Pacquets will all have 20 Guns ships if ye Warr with France continues.*

Despite enlargement and rearmament packets fell prey to the enemy. On the 25th March 1747, the **Eagle** (2), under Capt Boone, was taken prize in the Channel on her return passage from Jamaica, *by the* **Count de Maurapas** *Privateer of 16 Guns and 150 Men, and is carried into St. Maloes.* She was either quickly ransomed or replaced by another packet of the same name. The **Fawkener** (1) was taken twice, once in 1747 and again in the following year. On the first occasion she was retaken by British ships, and on the second, restored after being carried into Martinique.

On the outbreak of the Seven Years War, **Hanover** (2) was provided with 14 carriage guns of unknown poundage, but these proved insufficient to save her. During the second year of the war, in March 1757, she was taken prize by the French privateer **Count de Bentem**, and carried into Brest.

Perhaps the most unlucky packet of this war was the **General**

THE 'MERCURY' — FALMOUTH PACKET.
(From a painting on glass in possession of the Falmouth Municipality.)

The **Mercury**,
1778 – 81
*This stylised portrait of the packet **Mercury**, depicts an older style packet with a low 'beak-head', little different from those employed in the 1750s. Commanded by Capt Robert Dillon, the original portrait was painted on glass. It was in the possession of the Falmouth Town Council in the 1920s, but its current whereabouts (if it has survived) is unknown*

Wall. When she brought Benjamin Franklin to England in 1757, he noted that at one stage she had achieved 13 knots. Capt Kennedy, RN a passenger on board, contended that *no ship sailed so fast*. A wager was made and Kennedy himself cast the log, but *owned his wager lost*. Despite her potential speed, she was taken prize on three later occasions, each time while homeward bound from New York. Each time she was released for decreasing sums of ransom – first for £2,500 in March 1760, then for £600 in March 1761 and finally for £577 10s in May 1762. After this final episode her packet contract was cancelled.

American Revolution; or War of Independence

After the initial continental stages of the War for American Independence, the rebels took to the seas, carrying the war to Britain. Even so, while numerous American privateering actions were reported during 1776, it was February 1777 before the first of a string of packet losses occurred. The **Swallow** (2), outward bound for New York was the first, taken by the privateer **Reprisal**, on February 22nd 1777, while a month later, on the same route, the **Harriott** beat off a determined attack by the American privateer **Lee**, losing seven men in the process, and another nine wounded.

The general adoption of copper sheathing gave this generation of packets marginally more speed, but few could outsail their American opponents. There were however some noble defences. As a Falmouth packet the **Grenville** (2), a prize previously taken from the Spanish, was heavily beset on two or three occasions. An action against three American privateers, attributed to 1777, cannot be verified. However, on March 4th 1778, when approaching Barbados, she was attacked by, and successfully beat off, two American privateers. One of these being *a Rebel Brig of Eighteen Six pounders and 130 Men*. When the **Grenville** (2) arrived at Falmouth, her master reported that seven men had been wounded and one man killed in the action, and that *the established Capt. Kempthorne was so much wounded … that he is left behind in the* W Indies. The roof of Kempthorne's mouth had been shot away, but he made a good recovery. Even though the mails had been sunk during the fight, the PMG was later pleased to award:

> *… a considerable sum of money to the Captain and officers of the* **Grenville** *packet boat, and 10£. to each of the common sailors, for the gallant behaviour and bravery in an engagement for three hours with two American privateers at different times, and obliging them to sheer off.*

The actual sums awarded consisted of £100 to Capt Kempthorne, £50 to the mate who was also wounded, £20 to the Surgeon, £10 to each of seven wounded seamen and a guinea to each of the remaining seamen.

The following year she was again in close action. Lloyd's List of Tuesday October 19th 1779 reported:

> *The* **Grenville** *Packet Boat, Capt. Kempthorne, sailed from New York the 6th of September, and arrived at Falmouth the 13th Inst. She brings advice that the* **Mercury** *Packet Boat, Capt. Dillon, was arrived at New York with the Mail from England.*

> *The* **Grenville**, *on the 10th September, in her passage to England, in Lat. 40.00 N. Long. 72.28 W. fell in with three Rebel Privateers, viz. a Brig of 14 Guns, a Sloop of 14, and a Schooner of 10 Guns, which he beat off, after a severe Engagement of two Hours. The* **Grenville** *received six Shot between Wind and Water, and other Damage in her Hull; her Rigging and Sails were shattered to pieces; her Masts and Yards much damaged, and two Men wounded, one of them, the first Mate, had his right Eye shot out by a Piece of Iron of above Half a Pound Weight, which lodged in his Head, but was afterwards extracted.*

Such engagements were desperate affairs, and the above, if not typical, was not unusual. Her armament at that time is uncertain.

Despite PO disapproval, several packet owners obtained letters of marque during this conflict.

Packet	Rig	Tons	Carriage Guns	Swivel Guns	Men	Commander
Thynne	Ship	200	14 x 3-pdrs	8	50	Sampson Hall
King George (2)		200	14 x 6-pdrs	6	60	George Wauchope
Grantham	Ship	200	14 x 6-pdrs	6	58	James Bull
Halifax (2)	Brig	160	6 x 6-pdrs	none	60	John Boulderson Jnr

Between them they took several modest prizes – not all of then lawfully. The 100-ton, American brigantine **Thorn**, commanded by Philip Aubin, was advertised for sale at Falmouth in April 1781, together with her cargo of 83 hogsheads of molasses; three puncheons of rum and 6,000 lb of cotton wool. On checking the respective dates, it would appear that the **Thorn** had been seized before the **Grantham** was licensed to take prizes! No record of a letter of marque being issued for the packet **Duke of Cumberland**, has yet been discovered, but she too took at least one prize. The **Mary**, a *prize taken from the Colonials*, which was condemned in the High Court of Admiralty on March 4th 1783, and was later registered at Falmouth as a B*ritish built 60 ton brigantine*.

By its close in 1783, the American War of Independence had seen over twenty-nine packet engagements. Of these the packets only won five, but they had also taken a few prizes in their turn. In all twenty-four packets were taken by the enemy, nine of which were restored or later retaken, leaving fifteen packets irredeemably lost to the enemy. These cost the PO over £62,600 in compensation to the owners, while those which were retaken or restored cost a further undisclosed sum in salvage and repairs. It was partly because of this high level of losses that the PO was induced to become packet owners in their own right. Towards the end of this period they purchased thirteen packets at a cost of about £78,000, over half of these were later taken prize, and between them they cost around £22,000 in repairs and running charges. Wars were costly in so many ways.

Sloop or Smack 1820

9 War Losses: Privateers & Prizes 1793–1815

A few of the new standard packets had been brought into service before the French Revolutionary War commenced in 1793. Designed as fast sailers, their armament was initially limited to four 4-pounders ... *to keep off Row Boats and make Signals, and Small Arms for the men lest they should be boarded by any little Privateer ...*, along with two long 6-pounders as 'chasers'. While outright speed was important, it was only one factor, and many packet engagements took place in calm conditions. Despite the claims, there is little to indicate that these packets were significantly faster than their predecessors. As most commanders found their limited fire power unnerving, they soon found excuses to augment their weaponry.

Maltese Speronara 1830

Captain Yescombe's new packet **King George** (4) was armed with six 6-pounder cannon, when completed in 1796. Just two years later he changed her main armament to eight short 12-pounders, at his own expense. By which his vessel was:

> *... relieved from the greater weight, will sail faster & should she be overtaken the superior weight of shot which the short gun carries will enable her to make a better defence ...*

These eight *short guns* must have been carronades, so perhaps Yescombe was responsible for introducing them to the service – they proved a mixed blessing. Shorter and lighter than cannon, carronades discharged a greater weight of metal, but at the cost of range and accuracy. They were close quarters guns, designed to smash an enemy's hull. All of which tended to make them a good defensive weapon, but when Captain Mudge surrendered the **Queen Charlotte** (2) in May 1805, two of his carronades were out of action, and one of the three cannon on the engaging side, dismounted by an enemy shot. The local newspaper noted that:

> *The carronades now used in the packets are unfit for a long action. When they get warm, they recoil so violently, as to break their breachings, tackles, &c. and much time is consequently lost in repairing the mischief.*

Even so these carronades enabled Yescombe and the crew of the **King George** (4) to put up a gallant defence against the **Reprisaille** in 1803, but they were taken in the end, Yescombe later dying of his wounds. Such losses were not encouraging. When the new **Windsor Castle** arrived at Falmouth in August 1804, she was ...*most excellently fitted up, and has every accommodation to make passengers comfortable, pierced for 16 guns with better quarters for fighting than any packet in the service.* She never mounted sixteen guns, and at the time of her glorious action with **Le Jeune Richard** in 1807 (see Introduction and pp50–51), she mounted just six long 4-pounders and two 9-pound carronades. John Bull's **Duke of Marlborough**, (2) completed in 1806, was armed with six 12-pounder carronades, and four

Packet Identification Flags
In the early 1800s, if not before, packet identification flags were introduced to help identify individual packets while still a long way off shore. Besides the immediate family and friends of the crew, many others in Falmouth were interested in the safe return of a packet. To meet this interest cards, listing the current identification flags allocated to the different packets and their respective commanders, were printed commercially in a number of formats

FALMOUTH PACKETS' SIGNALS.
Published by J. Philp, Bookseller.

Packet List, 1827
This packet list, the key to the packet flags reproduced on the facing page, was published by J. Philip, of Falmouth, in his early guide book
A Panorama of Falmouth
(The Cornwall Centre)

Names and Commanders.

#	Name	Commander
1	Duke of Marlborough	Bull
2	Magnet	Porteous
3	Stanmer	Sutton
4	Sandwich	Schuyler
5	Goldfinch	Walkie
6	Lapwing	Forster
7	Hope	Wright
8	Spey	James
9	Osborne	Leslie
10	Nocton	Morphew
11	Sphynx	Passingham
12	Duke of York	Snell
13	Lord Melville	Webbe
14	Princess Elizabeth	Scott
15	Swallow	Baldock
16	Camden	Tilly
17	Lady Pelham	Cary
18	Frolic	Green
19	Eclipse	Griffin
20	Kingfisher	Walker
21	Rinaldo	Hill
22	Emulous	Croke
23	Cygnet	Gooding
24	Plover	W. Downey
25	Zephyr	Church
26	Wellington	Lugg
27	Sheldrake	Ede
28	Mutine	Pawle
29	Tyrian	Dwyer
30	Skylark	Peters
31	Pigeon	Binney
32	Opposum	Hannam
33	Barracouta	James
34	Lyra	St. John
35	Reynard	Dunsford
36	Calypso	Peyton
37	Briseis	I. Downey

Routes of the Packets.

ISLANDS.
From Falmouth to
Barbadoes
St. Lucie
Martinique
Dominique
Guadaloupe
Antigua
Montserrat
Nevis
St. Kitts
Tortola
St. Thomas
back to
Falmouth.

MEDITERN.
Falmouth
Cadiz
Gibralter
Malta
Corfu
Malta
Gibralter
Cadiz
Falmouth.

BRAZILS.
Jan. to June.
Falmouth
Madeira
Rio Janeiro
Bahia
Fernambuco
Falmouth
July to Decr.
Madeira
Teneriffe
Pernambuco.

Bahia
Rio Janeiro
Falmouth.

JAMACA & CARTHAGENA.
Falmouth
Barbadoes
St Vincent
Grenada
Jamaica
Carthagena
Jamaica
Crooked Island
Falmouth.

AMERICA.
Falmouth
Halifax
Bermuda
Halifax
Falmouth.

BUENOS AYRES
Falmouth
Rio Janeiro
Monte-Video
Buenos Ayres
Monte-Video
Rio Janeiro
Falmouth.

MEXICO.
Falmouth
St. Domingo
Jamaica
Vera Cruz
Tampico
Vera Cruz
Havannah
Falmouth.

Mails made up in London.

Lisbon every Tuesday ;—Mediterranean and Brazils first Tuesday in every month ;—Jamaica and Carthagena, and America, first Wednesday every month ;—Leeward Islands, and Jamaica and Mexico, third Wednesday every month ;—Buenos Ayres, third Tuesday every month. Those Packets whose Mails are made up on Tuesdays, sail from Falmouth on Friday morning; and those which are made up on Wednesday, on Saturday morning.

Mails for La Guayra are made up in London the first Wednesday in every month, and forwarded by the Jamaica Packet to Barbadoes, from whence it is taken to La Guayra by a Mail Boat, and that Boat meets the Island Packet at St. Thomas's.

Sold by J. PHILP, at the Falmouth Bazaar.

long 9-pounders – chase guns, a pair of each on the forecastle and poop. This combination seems to have been the official armament for established packets towards the end of these wars, the **Express** (1) being similarly armed in 1813.

However, firepower was not everything. A fiery spirit, dogged determination, or even a terrible fear of loosing, was often the deciding factor. When the old style packet **Antelope** was attacked by a large French schooner privateer, on December 1st 1793, few would have predicted the final outcome – the **Antelope** being armed with only six 3-pounder cannon while her attacker was the **Atalanta**, a French privateer of 8 guns and 65 men. After an all night chase, the **Antelope** was brought to action off Cuba. Homeward bound she was short-handed. Only twenty-three men were fit for service – Smith, the second mate and three seamen having died of a fever at Jamaica, while two on board were still ill.

Conditions were near calm when the **Atalanta** closed with her, and the **Antelope's** crew had had plenty of time to prepare for action, charging and shotting their small cannon and swivel guns, rigging the anti-boarding netting, drawing and loading their muskets, blunderbusses and pistols, and honing their boarding pikes and cutlasses. The action, when it commenced, was fast and furious Capt Curtis was killed in driving off the first boarding attempt, as was John Austin, the ship's steward, and a French gentleman passenger (aide-de-camp to Mons. Lapponet). The mate, Mr Bryan Mitchell, was shot through the body, rendering him unable to fight, leaving boatswain, John Pascoe to assume command and continue the action. In his own words:

> She then made another Attempt to board us by cutting down the Boarding Nettings, Ridge Ropes, etc., but they all got killed in the attempt. Our loss this Sally was three more wounded; but they then tried to get off by cutting their Grappling Rope but were prevented by the … lashing of her Square Sail Yard to our Fore Shrouds. We directly after found her Fire slacken which greatly encouraged Us. We kept up a constant Fire for half an hour more when we had the Pleasure of seeing them cry for Mercy, but to all appearance they deserved none nor expected any as some of them jumped overboard and drowned themselves, for their Bloody Flag was nailed to the Masthead. They were then ordered to take it down and we took possession.

Against all odds the packet had taken their attacker. In the action, 50 of the **Atalanta's** crew were either killed, missing or wounded, and of the packetmen, only two were killed and a few wounded, though the surgeon later died of *great fatigue*.

Heavily mauled, the **Antelope** returned to Jamaica with her prize, where a hero's welcome awaited them. The governor awarded 100 guineas to Mr Mitchell the mate, 100 guineas to the boatswain, and 100 guineas to the crew, as a reward for their gallantry.

On her return to England, the public's reaction was overwhelming. John Pascoe was singled out for special attention, including a gold boatswain's call. In addition, *the Committee for encouraging the Capture of French Privateers* made handsome awards to the crew and dependants. The PO had little choice but to emulate these, and also applied *to the Lords of the Admiralty to give up the Prize to the Captors though a droit of Admiralty.* However, the spirit of their awards was tempered by a strict rejoinder from the PMG:

> ... *let it be thoroughly understood amongst the Officers and their Crews that these Rewards are given only in consequence of the particular Circumstances attending this singular Action in which the Antelope was first chased from 9 O'clock AM December 1st till 2nd December when she was obliged to defend herself against an attack, but did not first attack an Enemy for the Post Master General by no means intend to depart from the Principle which they have been ordered to adopt of considering it to be the duty of the Packets to outsail the Enemy whenever they can & by no means to fight when it can possibly be avoided.*

One reason why the packets fared better than expected lay in a basic privateering tactic. The privateermen were regarded as little more then legitimised pirates, and their only reward lay in selling prize ships and cargoes, which they needed to take with as little material damage as possible. Well armed and heavily manned, they relied on the threat of havoc and slaughter as their main weapon, and many flew the 'bloody red flag', declaring no quarter. On approaching they tended to concentrate their fire into their opponents sails and rigging, to render them helpless. As a consequence casualties, on or below their opponents decks, were relatively low. If this demonstration of firepower and intimidation failed, the privateermen would finally board and try to carry their opponents by sheer weight of numbers.

The packetmen on the other hand were desperate to drive off, cripple or sink their attacker, they had no thoughts of prize money, only survival. And in the final moments, as the enemy massed to board, many a packet was saved by a timely discharge of grapeshot, or canister, cutting a swathe through the enemy, inflicting terrible carnage, and allowing the packet to work clear and escape.

Through the eyes of many latter-day historians the history of the Falmouth packets in action was a chequered one, at times illuminated by brilliant acts of bravery, and at others clouded by craven cowardice – but these were not fighting ships. Of course historians write from cover, assuming the traditions of British maritime supremacy. Assuming that the British bulldog spirit applied in every situation, and that the underdog, fighting against all odds should prevail. It certainly does happen; but in reality not very often.

In considering the packets' chequered wartime behaviour, one aspect should always be borne in mind – the conventions of war that pertained at the time. Throughout this era, officers and gentlemen were expected to behave in an honourable fashion. In recognition of this, conventions of behaviour were assumed if not formally agreed and codified, to prevent dishonour being forced upon a gentlemen.

One such convention was that a significantly inferior ship did not force a superior one to fight, as the superior vessel's inevitable victory carried no honour for her officers. This was invariably the position in which packet commanders found themselves when confronted by enemy warships. Against such odds, if the packet could not out sail her adversary, then her commander had no honourable recourse but to surrender after perhaps discharging a token gun.

A case in point concerns Capt Vivian and his temporary packet **Little Catherine**. Bermudan built, and a fast sailer in the right conditions, she was armed with… *the usual number of Guns and ammunition found and provided by his Majesty's Post Master General.* As per Capt Vivian's protest sworn on December 20th 1813 – after sailing for Falmouth on the 23rd November 1813 – she found herself opposed by a squadron of enemy vessels.

After running for four or five hours, Capt Vivian had no effective recourse but to surrender. However, his notions of honourable behaviour did not end with his capture. His crew, divided between the two frigates – **La Sultane** and **L'Etoile**; Captain Vivian and seventeen of his men found themselves held on board the former. Days later a gale sprang up, and the frigate (largely manned by elderly *invalides*) was in difficulties. Her commander asked Capt Vivian for his men's assistance – on their parole not to take advantage of the situation! This they did most effectively, returning to their confinement when the danger was past. On the 12th December, the frigate captured another packet, the **Duke of Montrose** (2) and in recognition of Vivian's honourable behaviour, she was given up to him and his crew, by which they returned to Falmouth and freedom.

Such notions of honour dictated the thoughts and actions of most regular naval officers, and packet commanders, but there was little sense of honour amongst privateermen. They were in it for the prize money.

Packet losses to enemy warships and privateers were particularly heavy during the final conflict with the British Americans. In many ways it was akin to civil war, with all the additional anguish as to rights and wrongs of fighting against friends and relatives. The need to be seen to do the right thing, and behave honourably weighed heavy with many packet captains. When the temporary packet **Morgianna** was taken on her maiden voyage, James Cunningham was most anxious to cover himself.

*This superior Privateer is called the **Saratoga** of New York, is nearly new,* *armed with 18 long Carriage guns … mostly 12-prs. with swivels, Muskettoons & blunderbusses & … 135 choice seamen …*

… not only their Lordships, but the world will say this contest was unequal & that no part of the British Character can be sullied by this surrender …

Friendly Fire

The graphic television images of the two Gulf Wars dramatically brought home the dangers of 'friendly fire'. At the time the media presented it as something new, but in fact it was a problem as old as war itself. Incidents of this kind between ships of the same nation were all too common, and throughout the protracted Revolutionary and Napoleonic wars, there were a number involving Falmouth packets.

During these wars the constant threat from enemy privateers created high levels of tension on board merchant vessels, and a great deal of suspicion of other shipping. On board the packets this tension was heightened by vociferous criticisms that a number of packets had been given up too easily. Such criticism led to many commanders putting up spirited, but almost foolhardy, defences.

As well as attacks by the enemy there were also occasional skirmishes between British privateers and the PO packets. These tended to be more alarming than serious, as unless the prize in prospect appeared a rich vessel, most privateers tended to shy away from heavy engagements. On the other hand, engagements with British warships were potentially disastrous, and there were a few!

Packets invariably tried to avoid contact with all suspicious shipping, but Royal Navy commanders had a duty to close with, and challenge the identity of all shipping encountered – save against grossly superior odds. And, while confidential recognition signals were commonplace, their extension to include HM Packets was at first discounted. In February 1793, the Board of Admiralty considered:

The Signal at present Established to distinguish the Packet Boats (an English Jack hoisted at the Fore Top Gal.t Mast head) is considered by their Lordships as sufficient for the above purpose for the present

By the early 1800s, individual packet recognition flags had been adopted by the commanders at Falmouth, and on approaching port they were to display a … *White Jack at the main-top-gallant masthead – an English ensign at the peak – and the distinguishing flag of your ship at the fore-top-gallant masthead.* Printed cards listing the packets, their commanders and their respective identification flags were published commercially and several examples survive (see pp76/77).

About the same time confidential private recognition signals were introduced for exchange between PO packets and RN ships. Comprising day and night signals, these consisted of seven sets of challenges and answers – one for each day of the week. The sets of signals were fixed for a period of weeks or months, but their assignment to specific days was frequently changed – of which, hopefully, all authorised holders of sets of signals were duly advised, while the enemy remained ignorant.

Unlike the packet identification flags, the security of these confidential signals was of high concern. Those issued to packet commanders had lead weighted covers, and in any likelihood of an enemy taking a packet, the confidential Book of Signals was to be thrown overboard and sunk, along with the mail. Officers issued with a set of signals were accountable for their safe return, or furnishing a suitable explanation if and when lost. As William Gay, the agent's deputy at Falmouth, assured Francis Freeling in December 1813:

> Sir, I beg to inform you in answer to Mr. Clarkes's Letter of the 27th instant, that the Private Signals of the **Little Catherine** and **Duke of Montrose** Packets, their Commanders inform me, were sunk with the Mails when they were captured by the Enemy.

While necessary, these signals could prove difficult to read at sea. Holding the weather-gage was a key naval tactic, and vessels usually attacked from the windward. Under these conditions any signal flags hoisted tended to blow directly towards, or away from, approaching vessels. And, viewed virtually end-on, these signal flags were often indistinguishable, which resulted in a number of unfortunate incidents.

In August 1801, outward bound with the West India mails, the packet *Penelope* was chased for some hours by a suspicious vessel, in 'privateer alley', to windward of Barbados. On board the packet the perceived danger was so real that the mailbags for Barbados had already been consigned to the deep, before the vessel was identified as HM sloop-of-war *Plover* – just in time to prevent the bags for Jamaica following suit.

As the RN vessels were invariably the challengers, one might have expected them to have assumed a greater 'duty of care', but sailing under false colours was a common 'ruse de guerre', and the smaller naval sloops could not afford to hold fire for too long. During another incident Captain Kidd's packet *Princess Elizabeth* (1), exchanged fire with HM sloop *Acteon*, when her commander failed to answer the private signals. Although no one was seriously injured, the packet was somewhat damaged. On this occasion the PO paid for the repairs, *instead of agitating the Question with the Lords of the Admiralty.* It was clearly a touchy subject.

And again, in April 1812, when the packet *Nocton* and HMS *Psyche* had an *unfortunate mistake relative to packets signals.* Very unfortunate for the surgeon of the packet, as a shot from the warship passed through his cabin, causing severe splinter wounds to his head. As a result of which, not surprisingly, *his faculties since have been totally deranged.*

However, most notorious of these incidents was a running fight, lasting two and a half hours, between HM brig **Primrose** and HM packet **Duke of Marlborough** (2) in March 1814. The full story of this fight has been told by Commander John Beck in his book *Captain John Bull,* but suffice it to say that the commander of the naval brig, Phillott, never attempted to make the private signal, as:

> ... *from the small proportion of sail she had set, and her whole Appearance, I, as well as my Officers, concluded her to be a Merchant Vessel, and during the whole subsequent Chase, I had not the least reason to alter my Opinion; and as my orders contain Information of several Privateers in the vacinity of my Cruise, it appeared very probable she was a captured Vessel, in which case it never appeared necessary to make the Private Signal.*

Both the appropriate day and night signals were made by the packet commander during the chase, but allegedly neither was observed from the naval brig. The brig, after firing a number of warning shots, eventually hauled close and opened fire in earnest. This the packet returned with equal vigour. Eventually, the *packet being almost a complete wreck,* the naval commander hailed her, and at last realised his mistake. It was a costly one. On board the packet one passenger (Lieutenant Adjutant Andrews of the 60th Regiment) was killed, three seamen severely wounded, and another eight slightly wounded. On board the naval brig, three hands were killed, or later died of their wounds, and a further twelve severely wounded. The disparity in the 'butcher's bills' is partly accounted for by the higher density of men on board HM ships.

An 18-gun sloop, HM brig **Primrose** mounted sixteen 32-pounder carronades – 'smashers', two long 6-pounders, and one 12-pound carronade on the forecastle, and had a compliment of 125 men while the **Duke of Marlborough** (2) mounted six 12-pounder carronades, together with four long 9-pounders, and was manned by a crew of 30, plus nine passengers.

Commander Phillott was later tried by court martial, where despite the loss of life and damage, the court merely *adjudged the said Capt. Phillott to be admonished to be more circumspect in future.*

A final incident of this kind was also one of the last packet actions of the war. On January 21st 1815, the packet **Queen Charlotte** (2), twenty days out of Guadeloupe for Falmouth and under the command of Captain Kirkness, fell in with HM brig **Harlequin**. Following the signing of the Treaty of Ghent, on December 24th 1814, Britain and the USA were technically at peace, but neither commander was aware of this fact. They approached each other warily, and unfortunately, the private signals not being recognised, there was a brisk exchange of fire before the mistake was appreciated. During that brief exchange the first lieutenant of the brig was killed and another hand wounded!

By the close of the Napoleonic war the Falmouth packets had been engaged by an enemy at least 128 times, including those where the packets put up no resistance. In these 44 were totally lost to the enemy, and 31 were retaken or restored after the fight. Thirty-five successfully fought off their attackers, and eight actually turned the tables and captured them. Taken in the round this was an impressive record for this fleet of little ships.

Rio de Janeiro Passage
Boat 1830

10 Mail, Passengers & Freight

Mail

The mail portmanteau was the last thing to be brought on board at the outset of a packet voyage, and the first thing to be landed at its end. In peacetime one of the small compartments, on the orlop under the cabin, was probably used to stow the mail, but in wartime the mail was kept on deck. The military, political and/or commercial disasters that might arise from an interception of the mails dictated that it was better for them to be lost than taken. Duplicate copies of all important dispatches and commercial correspondence were invariably forwarded by the next packet, to guard against any such potential loss. On board the packets, steps were taken to ensure that, in moments of potential defeat, the mails could be instantly jettisoned and sunk. This meant keeping them on deck at all times, and to protect the mails from the worst effects of wind and weather they were packed in custom-made portmanteaus.

Barque-rigged Packet 1835

Made of stout leather, well dressed to render them as waterproof as possible, the same portmanteaus were used on both coach journeys (between London and Falmouth), and on packet voyages. Made in three sizes, the largest were five feet long, by one foot ten inches across the ends. Heavily stitched and stapled, with stout carrying handles, these cost about £5 each. They suffered heavy wear and tear on deck, because *although covered with a tarpaulin, no care can prevent the portmanteaus getting wet.* While the Falmouth office took great pains to prolong their life, they had to endure climatic extremes ranging from equatorial heat, to near arctic cold, and worst of all the steaming humidity of the tropics.

> *In the winter they are carefully dried by the fire, looked over and repaired, and in the summer they are hung out of doors, but it frequently happens from the heat of the sun in a tropical climate and the exposure to seawater as before mentioned, that a new portmanteau is spoiled and rotten in a single voyage.*

To ensure that the mails did in fact sink, when jettisoned, each portmanteau was weighted at the commencement of each voyage with two or more heavy iron pigs, provided by the PO for the purpose. Even the biggest ones could be manhandled by one or two men, and before a packet went into action the weighted portmanteaus were hung over the stern, or the side – ready to be cut away and sunk in an instant.

Occasionally they were shot away in action and lost by mistake, but on only a few occasions did a jettisoned portmanteau float ignominiously, and fall into enemy hands. When this happened the commander had to answer to a committee of his fellow captains.

Gentlemen,

I now appear before you, as the late Commander of the Temporary Packet **Mary Ann** *to answer for my conduct, in my late encounter with an American Privateer (***General Tompkin***, April 8th 1813); and by which, after an action of One Hour and half (Forty five minutes of which was within Musquet Shot) the Packet was captured…*

The Minutes of the Action have already been deliver'd to the President of this Court…

… I have now to allude to the floating of the Mails after they were thrown overboard – Being young in the Service of the Post Office I had never heard of an instance where the Portmanteau had floated; and had I not conceived that the Two Piggs of Iron, I had received from the Store for the purpose of sinking the Mails, would have been sufficient I should have made an application for more; and should in that case have had nothing to regret but the loss of the Ship.

On Commissioning the **Mary Ann** *at this Port in August 1811; I received (with various stores from this office) Two Piggs of Iron Ballast to sink the mails with the weights of which you are well acquainted – In my first Voyage to the West Indies I had Four Portmanteaus, (two of which were small ones) since that period, have had more and at times less, and at the Capture had Two: It was therefore natural for me to suppose; that as two Piggs were given me for the purpose of sinking the Mails; and that those often consisted of more than one Portmanteau; that a Pigg of Iron was sufficient to sink one of these and under this impression I had no doubt when the Mails were thrown over that they would have instantly sunk: but to my great Mortification and Chagrin they floated and were taken possession of by the Enemy.*

By this statement Gentlemen, you will perceive there was no wilful neglect or mismanagement in that respect, as no doubt could possibly have existed in my mind of the sufficiency of the weight –

My conduct therefore on this occasion, I cheerfully submit to your investigation: and from your candour and Justice have no doubt of the result; on which will depend my Character as an Officer; and the realizing or entirely disappointing of my future prospects in the Service –

Jas Caddy

The forgoing report is part of James Caddy's defence presented to a Committee of Captains, as reported by Saverland on May 31st 1813 (see report of Committee of Captains p127). Caddy (a half-pay Master, RN) was exonerated and given command of the **Swiftsure** on July 17th 1813.

In addition to their main salary, packet commanders were able to supplement their income from two other legitimate sources – the carriage of passengers and the shipment of *bullion on freight*. No such opportunities presented themselves to the other officers or seamen, apart from a few tips and crumbs falling from the cabin table. As the PO received a significant income from both, these activities were positively encouraged. But, to ensure that all was above board, each packet commander was required to make a *true return* of all passengers and bullion carried in their vessel at the end of every voyage. On each passenger the PO (for the Crown), received £4 per head at first – irrespective of the route travelled or the fare paid. And on the bullion they received one-third of the freight money paid for Lisbon bullion shipments, and two-thirds of that paid for transporting bullion across the Atlantic. These became significant sums.

Throughout the packet era, the most passengers were carried on the Lisbon route, as too (prior to the close of the Napoleonic Wars), was most of the bullion. But, as the senior commanders pointed out to the PMG when their earnings were declining in 1818:

> ... *the depreciation since the Peace has been greater on the Lisbon Station than on any other,* ...

> ... *Mr. Saverland's return of Passengers carried by our Ships, which will shew that in the last Year we have not carried so many by One Hundred and Seventy Three as in the preceding one, and our Freight of Bullion has decreased in much greater proportion; nor are the emoluments of our Station likely to return ... the Court of Portugal being removed to the Brazils, has drawn with it the Commercial Interest of Lisbon, on which your Lordships must be well aware that our Profit chiefly depends.*

> *We cannot doubt your Lordships consider the Lisbon Station a reward for long Service.*

The Lisbon route might have declined, but only proportionally, and the South American routes offered new possibilities – to the junior commanders! And, following the establishment of the Mexican packets in 1826, the additional freights of bullion on that route more than made up for any earlier overall losses.

Passengers

Packet travel was relatively expensive. The fare from England to the West Indies, set in 1703 at £12, had risen to £50 by 1803. But high costs did not prevent large numbers of passengers from travelling by the packets. There was a steady demand from statesmen, diplomats, state officials and messengers; officers and gentlemen; traders and merchants. Each, occasionally accompanied by their wives and families, sought berths to and from Falmouth and destinations spread around the Atlantic rim, and throughout the Mediterranean. We don't know how many travelled by packet before the last quarter of the eighteenth century, but it was clearly significant, and was covered in all known packet contracts. By mid-century large numbers of emigrants were moving from Britain to North America – mainly via London, Bristol and Liverpool. Few of these could afford mail packet travel, and of several thousand transatlantic travellers listed in Fothergill's *Emigrants*

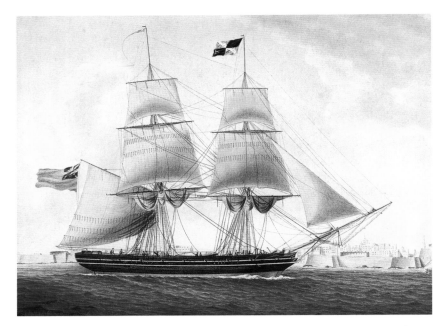

The **Swiftsure**,
1812–23
Built at Fowey in 1812,
the **Swiftsure** was
employed from new as a
temporary packet to
cover war time losses.
Later established as a
regular packet, she is
depicted here by
Cammillieri entering
Malta in 1817, when
under the command of
James Caddy. As she
only undertook one
Mediterranean voyage
in 1817, which occupied
from January 29th to
April 14th, she must
have been at Malta
between the end of
February and early
March. Antonio
Espinoza, the Director of
the Malta Maritime
Museum, has discovered
that Cammillieri did not
return from Marseilles
until early in 1817, so
this must have been one
of his first ship portraits
painted after his return
from exile (NMMC)

from England: 1773–76, only five are listed against Falmouth packets. Possibly only one of these was a true emigrant – Colin Campbell, who sailed from Falmouth for Carolina on January 20th 1774, aboard the **Lord LeDespencer**. At least two of the five were travellers – Robert Bogle, a 50 year old Londoner, travelling *on his business* from Falmouth to Grenada on board the packet **Anna Teresa**, in February 1774, and Robert Henson, of St Vincent, *on his return home from a visit to his friends in England*, by the same packet.

From later 'head money' returns to the PO we have a better idea of the numbers of passengers travelling by packets after 1773. Over the next 40 years passenger numbers climbed dramatically from 230 in 1774, to 1,864 in 1814. The returns generally indicate more people travelled homewards to Britain in the packets than outwards, reflecting the better opportunities for outward bound voyagers by regular merchant vessels sailing from other British ports.

The Falmouth packets offered two classes of passenger travel – cabin and steerage. While superior cabin passengers might commandeer the captain's saloon, the regular cabin passengers berthed in six lightly timbered hutches, three on either side of the ship. Little more than six foot long by four foot wide, each contained one or two narrow single bunks, and was located close to the water line. There were no external portholes, and the only natural light filtered from the mess-room skylight, through a dark glass bull's-eye let into each cabin door. For a long time 12 cabin bunks seems to have been the maximum number provided, though there were frequently more passengers than berths. The steerage passengers apparently berthed in the common mess-room, probably sleeping in cots or hammocks. When the **Grenville** left the West Indies in 1781, she carried 20 passengers. The steward and boys:

> ... had daily two dinners to prepare as the Earl (of Harrington), with a select party, had a mess in the cabin, and the planters, merchants, etc., were confined wholly to the steerage or mess-room, from which latter class, the Earl occasionally invited some to partake at his table.

The voyage home was quite protracted, and as the water ran short:

> We were put to an allowance of three pints of water each man per diem, except the passengers. The ship's candles were expended long before the passage ended, and were under obligation to the Earl for wax candles to burn in the bittacle. Train oil was used in the mess-room in a lamp which was suspended over the arm chest.

And amongst the other passengers was:

> ... a Jew named Levi, who was going to London to have a cancer cut from his under lip, on which he wore a black plaster, and sat at the table in the steerage with the other passengers, selecting such victuals only as he chose to eat, some of which was provided wholly by himself, viz: Jew beef salted and spiced, each piece having a lead ticket fastened to it; he had also a large quantity of rusk and sweet cakes, and always drank out of his own cup on account of his cancer.   (Samuel Kelly, 1781)

It was a busy period, and although the **Grenville** (2) was chock full by transatlantic standards, a staggering 46 passengers were brought home from Lisbon, in the packet **Howe** in November 1792 – the largest number so far discovered to have been carried on any one voyage.

The fighting was over when army Lieutenant John Enys was ordered to join his regiment in Canada in 1784. Hoping for a home posting this was a ... *voyage to which I had no Inclination (but) was at length obliged to comply and having made all preparations necessary... procured a passage on board the* **Speedy** *packet then under Orders for Quebec.*

On arrival at Falmouth he tried to make final arrangements for his voyage, and although Capt D'Auvergne was out of town, Enys was pleased to learn from the Agent, and ... *everyone we spoke to that the Captain was a very agreeable young man and having learned that the Price was forty Guineas to be paid before embarkation we again returned to Truro.*

As far as can be ascertained, this was the same **Speedy** that had been captured off Barbados in July 1782 – since recaptured and returned to service. Measuring about 330 tons burthen, she was much larger than the normal run of packets, and as such would have had marginally superior accommodation. Although Enys does not describe his cabin in his journals, a mock-up has been created in the National Maritime Museum Cornwall, Falmouth.

Falmouth Packet List

TO MAY 28.
ORDER OF SAILING.

For *Lisbon*, every Friday, from April to October.
For *Barbadoes* and *Jamaica*, and *America*, on the Sunday after the first Wednesday in every month.
For *Surinam*, &c. on the Sunday after the second Wednesday in every month.
Leeward Islands, on the Sunday after the third Wednesday in every month.
Brazils, on the Saturday after the first Tuesday in every month.

NAMES	CAPTS.	Destin.	Sailed	Retrn
P. Elizabeth	Kidd	Lisbon	Mar. 23	May12
Marlbro'	Bull	Lisbon	April 23	May15
D. of Kent	Cotesworth	Coruna	May 18	
Arabella	Porteous	Lisbon	May 18	
P. Ernest	Petre	Lisbon	May 22	
Q. Charlotte	Mudge	Lisbon	May 18	
D. Kent 2	Lawrence	Lisbon	April 18	May16
F. Freeling	Bell	America	Dec. 22	May22
W. Castle	Sutton	Leew. I.	Feb. 23	
Prss. Mary	Pocoke	Surinam	Feb. 23	
L. Hobart	Hodge	Mediter.	Mar. 2	
Sandwich	Schuyler	Brazils	May 24	
Chichester	Rogers	Leew. I.	April 30	
Nocton	Naylor	Brazils	Sept. 6	Mar16
Townshend	Cock	Mediter.	Mar. 18	
Manchester	Elphinston	Halifax	Mar. 23	
L. Emily	Graham	Jamaica	Mar. 23	
L. Pelham	Stevens	Coruna	May 1	May16
Hichinbroke	James	Jamaica	May 18	
P. Charlotte	White	Leew. I.	Jan. 29	May17
Montagu	Norway	Mediter.	April 8	
Walsingham	Bullocke	Surinam	May 2	
Carteret t	Davey	Surinam	Jan. 19	May11
P. Elizab 2 t	Forresdale	Surinam	Mar. 23	
Chesterfield t	Hale	Brazils	Mar 23	
Express t	Quick	Brazils	Jan. 14	May19
Elita t	Stevens	Leew. I.	Mar. 31	
Darlington t	Harvey	Jamaica	Jan. 11	May13
Q Charlotte t	Kirkness	Lee. I.	May 28	
Montrose t	Blewett	America	May 28	
Diana t	Parsons	Jamaica	Dec 17	April
Adventure t	Sampson	Brazils	April 12	
Ann t	Britton	Jamaica	April 13	taken.
Speedy t	Sutherland	Bermuda	Feb. 23	
Mary Ann t	Caddy	Mediter.	Jun 9	taken.
Nymph t	Birsay	Mediter.	May 28	
Fox t	Tilly	Cadiz	May 1	
Swiftsure t	Furze	Brazils	Feb. 23	
Lapwing t	Ellsworthy	Mediter.	Feb. 23	
Catharine t	Vivian	America	April 18	

Falmouth Packet List Local newspapers featured weekly lists of current packet movements. At the height of the Napoleonic Wars, over 40 packets (established and temporary) were employed at any one time. Many were lost due to enemy action (The Cornwall Centre)

Off the Grand Banks in 20 days, Enys' passage to Quebec took 39 days to complete – their rate of travel varying from spending one 48 hour spell becalmed off Ushant, to a short period abreast of Cap des Rosiers (on the eastern curl of the Gaspé Peninsula), when the ship was going 13 Knots. *Capt. D'Auvergne could not believe this and went on deck himself to Look (at) the Logg when he made her Way to be twelve and a half Knotts.*

Organized entertainment on board was non-existent, and the passengers had to pass their time as best they could. Ensign Henry (1814) took … *an ample stock of books from home, and in the heat of the day, I either climbed up to the masthead and read there, or lounged under the cool of the awning.* Many travellers kept fulsome journals and read books, while others established card schools. *Our steerage mess was in the habit of card playing to a late hour, and for enormous sums of money; the loss and gain I think was sometimes from two to three hundred dollars (then £50–£75), 'till the captain forbade it.*

The only place for exercise was on deck, but even here there was little free space, what with the packet's carriage guns, boats, livestock housing, stowage of excess gear, and of course the constant movements of the crew working the ship.

On the Lisbon station passengers' provisions were all found by the commanders, but on the West Indian and American routes they were provided on the outward passage only, and homeward bound transatlantic passengers had to lay in their own sea-stock. Cabin fare on all routes was of the best, but with the average Lisbon passage taking less than a fortnight, relatively fresh food was constantly available. On these packets, commanded as they were by the senior established captains, the passengers were wined, dined and otherwise entertained right royally. Diplomatic, cultural and business relations with Portugal were strong throughout the packet era, and many of the Lisbon packet commanders attracted such a personal following that their packets were often full to bursting. As Captain Yescombe wrote in December 1792, *I am just about to sail with three and twenty cabin passengers & a King's Messenger for Spain…*

In a later period, and an altogether bigger vessel all round, accommodation was still very tight on board HM packet brig **Crane**, when she sailed for Rio in September 1850. It was her final outward voyage as a packet, and some 30 passengers required passage, including 15 miners, five wives and five children. This made the steerage accommodation so crowded, that her commander was obliged to share £45 *among the seamen to induce them to give up a part of their accommodation.*

While detailed accounts of packet travel are few and far between, a broad picture of patterns of travel during the first decade of the nineteenth century is revealed by the local newspapers. The embryo *Cornwall Gazette*, and its successor the *Royal Cornwall Gazette*, frequently published lists of names of cabin-class travellers, apparently furnished by the proprietors of either Wynn's Hotel, or Selley's Green bank Hotel – both of which establishments prospered during the packet era. Although the information published is far from complete – editions are missing, by no means was every voyage reported, and they seldom ever record steerage class passengers – these lists can be considered a fair minimum return of the cabin class passengers travelling.

Between March 1801 and January 1810, allowing for an eight-month break in publications between October 1802 and July 1803, 2,917 persons were noted as having travelled by the Falmouth packets. After January 1810 the lists fizzle out, but during that first decade of the nineteenth century it is possible to pick out many dignitaries, and regular travellers. Of those passengers noted, 2,445 were male; 360 female; and 112 children. Despite the hiatus of 1807–8, during most of which the Iberian Peninsula was closed to British shipping because of the French occupation, the most popular routes were those to Lisbon and the Spanish ports – 1,316 passengers. Another 870 people travelled to and from the West Indies during this period, with a further 402 people travelling to and from North America – again despite a general embargo on British shipping in US ports for part of the time.

In addition two new routes were opened during this decade. The first, to the Mediterranean, via Gibraltar, was pioneered by the **Lord Cornwallis** in February 1806, and the other was opened by the **Walsingham** (2) (displaced from the Lisbon service), in July 1808, to serve the Portuguese government in exile in Brazil. In the period covered, 280 people travelled to and from the Mediterranean, which was to become one of the more popular routes, while another 49 undertook the tedious Brazil voyage.

Twenty-four passengers came home from North America by the **Princess Mary** in June 1808, one of the largest numbers from this period. Taking just 19 days from Halifax, this was a swift passage, and despite the congestion the passengers were delighted with Captain Harvey's hospitality. They published their thanks:

The passengers arrived at Falmouth, in the packet **Princess Mary**, *from New York, via Halifax, take this method of expressing their joint and cordial thanks to Captain James Harvey, (acting), for his gentlemanly and polite treatment of them while on board. They feel a pleasure in this public expression of their high opinion of his conduct and professional abilities, and will always retain the most sincere interest in his welfare and prosperity. Signed on behalf of the whole passengers.*

William Graham

Matthew Moncrieff Pattison

People of substance were frequently travelling abroad for the benefit of their health. Amongst them was Exeter barrister Mr John Lyon, who, accompanied by his daughter, took passage for Lisbon on board the **Lord Auckland**, on September 28th 1806. Unfortunately it was to no avail. Less than three months later John Lyon died in Portugal, and his distraught daughter returned to England alone, disembarking at Falmouth on December 5th, from the **Prince of Wales** (2).

While the passenger trade was most active during the wars, not all the passengers arriving at Falmouth were welcome guests. Amongst others, the *Cornwall Gazette* of the 6th August 1803, reported the arrival from Lisbon *of a Spanish gentleman and servant*, by the **Duke of York** (3). Now whether he was a spy or a political refugee or whatever this anonymous Spanish gentleman was deemed an undesirable alien. A reward was offered, but there were no subsequent reports that he was taken, nor any indication of his cause of offence.

Much more welcome were the diplomatic passengers, the governors and ambassadors, with their entourages. Their liberal means of travel meant that their arrival was eagerly anticipated, though their stay at Falmouth was often brief. On Saturday April 18th 1801, the Marquis de Pombeira, and his suite of 15 persons, arrived at Wynn's Hotel, sailing the following morning in the **Walsingham** (2), for Lisbon. These were heady days when Falmouth was the staging point for international diplomacy. The **King George** (4) arrived at Falmouth from Lisbon on August 27th 1802, having on board Baron Slaten, the Russian ambassador to the court of Portugal, along with the Portuguese consul for St Petersburg, his secretary and a messenger. Also on board was one Mr Wright, physician to his Royal Highness the Duke of Sussex, whose affairs of the heart in Portugal were causing political palpitations in Whitehall. While these arrivals were normally joyful occasions, with accompanying civic receptions and other social activities, it was not always so.

On the 10th of October 1801, Charles Arbuthnot, Esq., British Consul General at Lisbon arrived on board the **Prince of Wales** (2) with his family. Theirs had been a most distressing passage. His daughter of five months, Caroline Emma, was ill to the point of death, and may

FALMOUTH.
TEN GUINEAS REWARD.

IT having been represented at the Alien Office in London, that an Alien named JOSEPH DE GOMES was landed at Falmouth, on or about the 31st of July last, in violation of the Alien Act, and is supposed to be secreted in or near Falmouth; and the Rev. PHILIP WEBBER, mayor of Falmouth, and one of his Majesty's Justices of the Peace for the county of Cornwall, having been requested by the Secretary of State to use his utmost endeavours to discover and apprehend the said Alien: a REWARD of TEN GUINEAS will, in consequence thereof, be paid by the Mayor of Falmouth, to any person or persons giving information where the said JOSEPH DE GOMES is secreted, so that he may be apprehended and brought before him, or any of his Majesty's Justices of the Peace for the said county. And all masters of ships are hereby cautioned against taking the said Alien out of the kingdom, as by the late Alien Act they will in such case incur a heavy penalty.

The said JOSEPH DE GOMES is about 5 feet 11 inches high, of a dark copper-colour complexion, has lost one or more of his fore teeth, and has dark hair tied without powder.

JAMES TIPPET, Town-clerk.
Falmouth, 20th September, 1803.

'De Gomes' Alien
This wanted notice was published in the Royal Cornwall Gazette on Saturday August 6th 1803. It was a comparatively rare notice and gave no reason as to why he was a 'wanted man'
(The Cornwall Centre)

even have died during the voyage – being buried at Falmouth on October 13th.

In May 1802, some unusual passengers arrived on board the **Walsingham** (2), in the form of a flock of 50 fine Merino sheep. A breeding flock *of the true Spanish breed*, for Lord Somerville. *They are of a small size, and are esteemed for their wool.* While not exactly contraband goods, it is not quite certain just how such shipments could be squared with the no trading rules, but perhaps they were diplomatic sheep!

The PO gained appreciably from the packet passengers. While the commanders kept the major part of the fares, they had to cover all the overheads, as well as passing on the head money on each passenger. Initially set at £4 per head, this was increased about 1795 to four guineas, and again about 1811 to five guineas. By the close of the Napoleonic wars it had become a significant sum, and during the peak year of 1813, the PO received nearly £10,000 in head money alone from the Falmouth packets. However, the packet service was already feeling the pinch for passengers on the North American route, and more and more service personnel were travelling by warships and stores-ships – all bigger vessels with superior accommodation and better food. The economics of running a packet were becoming quite marginal, and whereas the commanders had previously been able to absorb excess costs, by ... *the fortuitous influx of Passengers and Freight money*, these sources which were now both declining (see rates for Passengers pp128–30).

Freight of Bullion

During the eighteenth century, that other legitimate commodity – bullion – was mainly carried on the Lisbon route. But, as the nineteenth century unfolded, the value of gold and silver from the New World increased dramatically to become pre-eminent.

From the earliest times the Admiralty permitted naval warships to carry bullion and treasure, and later on there was great competition between regular Naval vessels and the packets for bullion freights. On the 26th of February 1834, HM sloop **Columbine**, arrived at Portsmouth from Havana:

> ... having quitted it that day month. She called at most of the ports on the Spanish Main, to try for freight to England, but apparently the merchants have taken a prejudice to shipping their money in men-of-war, owing to the detention which very frequently takes place by the ships putting into the different ports, and not getting to England for months after the money has been shipped; such detention being a serious injury to the consignees, in addition to having to pay a higher rate of premium.
>
> The **Gannet** and **Columbine** have each returned without freight, although there was plenty to send home, for the two Post-office packets, **Pigeon** and **Lady Mary Pelham**, were loaded with upwards of a million dollars, in presence of the **Columbine**.

The carriage of bullion on freight was no latter-day phenomenon. Quite soon after the Lisbon service was established the high speed, frequency and diplomatic immunity from search of the packet boats made them attractive for carrying the bullion exported from Portugal in settlement of its trading debts.

Between 1729 and 1731, the Falmouth to London haulage contractor (Fry) brought up bullion from the packets worth in excess of £636,000, which paid him nearly £1,200 a year. This all came from Lisbon, and assuming the later rate of one-half a per cent as then current, this paid freight of £3,180. Of this the PO received about £1,060, while the four established packet commanders and their investors shared about £2,120. Each commander receiving about £132 10s. per annum, exclusive of any part of the packet's share due to them, being appreciably more than their mid-century annual salary of £78.

During the second half of the eighteenth century transatlantic bullion freights began to increase. They still lagged well behind those carried to and from Lisbon, but the gap was closing. Between 1780 and 1809, bullion freights in excess of £3.75M were carried by the Lisbon packets. Whereas, by comparison, for the first two decades of that period the transatlantic bullion freights did not exceed £0.28M

However, by 1800–09 these had increased to about £0.75M. Bullion freights from Lisbon almost dried up after the fall of Portugal in November 1807, and while the service was re-instated in October 1808, during the following decade transatlantic bullion freights consistently exceeded those of the Lisbon packets. With the establishment of the Portuguese Court in Exile in Brazil and the opening of the route to Rio de Janeiro, along with extending the Jamaica route to Carthgena, near the isthmus of Panama, transatlantic bullion freights advanced dramatically to exceeded £1.1M between 1810 and 1815.

Bullion freight rates varied according to the packet route. The Falmouth agent's accounts for 1785/6 to 1790/1 show that the Lisbon and transatlantic bullion freight accounts were kept separate. On the Lisbon packets the consignees paid the road haulage charges from Falmouth to London, and freight was charged a-half of one per cent of the gross value of the bullion. On the transatlantic routes land carriage charges were paid by the commanders out of the gross freight money received, and while freight charges on the New York route were increased from one, to one-and-a-half per cent, during this period, on the more risky West Indian routes, they were increased from one to two per cent.

Allowing for a nine-month break in the five year run of data, the accounts record over £1.6 million being carried by the Lisbon packets during this period, and over £711,000 by the transatlantic packets – in all over £2.3M.

The freight earnings of individual commanders differed widely across the service, but the spread during the above period seems typical for most of the second half of the eighteenth century. Ignoring the question of shares held in the packets, over the five years 1785/6 to 1790/91 the four senior commanders on the Lisbon route received £556 each on average (ranging from £623 for Capt Braithwaite of the **Hampden**, and the **Howe** – her direct replacement, down to £459 for Capt Todd of the **Hanover** (5)). Of the 17 transatlantic packets returning with bullion during this period, six of them were PO owned. And, while the 11 commanders of the contract hired packets received £255 7s each on average – the commanders of the six PO owned packets only received about £97 10s giving a clear indication of the relative worth of the Lisbon service, and a drawback of being employed directly by the PO.

By the early nineteenth century the picture had changed considerably. During the last quarter of 1811, 17 transatlantic packets brought home gold and silver valued at over £300,000. The net freight paid on which amounted to £4,985 14s 1d – of which the PO received £1,555 13s 7d and the packet commanders £3,430 0s 6d. This gave each commander a little over £200 per voyage on average, of which, even after the deduction of wagon freight charges to London, about £100 was retained by the commander, and £100 was divided amongst the packet's shareholders. This being worth about £300 per annum, to the junior commanders, on top of their current annual salary of £104.

Taking these figures as a fair average for the whole of 1811, even excluding the Lisbon freights, these yielded a gross annual sum of about £20,000, on bullion worth over £1.3M.

The Lisbon route still had its attractions, but the balance of earnings had now been redressed. During 1811–12 a Lisbon commander might have earned £579 (£104 salary, £428 from passengers and £47 from bullion freight), but a transatlantic commander could now have earned £958 (£104 salary, £167 from passengers, £687 from bullion freight) (see Account of Freight p130).

Bullion landed at Falmouth was conveyed to London by a succession of different carriers. By the turn of the eighteenth century Russell & Co, of Exeter, were the main hauliers, employing six horse or eight horse wagons. Proceeding at a walking pace of two to three miles an hour, and escorted by armed militia, these lumbering wagons took the best part of six days to complete their journey. Despite this length of time on the road, throughout the history of the service there were only one or two successful bullion robberies.

As the packets rarely came alongside the quays at Falmouth, the bullion had to be landed in boats. A risky process that required close supervision. From 1816 Russell's agent at Falmouth was Richard Courtis, and his duties entailed working in all weathers: *It has blown here a most dreadful gale of wind all day with rain, & I have been in the midst of it on the beach landing the last mentioned dollars.* Silver dollars formed a major part of the bullion shipments in that period.

In the opening years of the nineteenth century Russells replaced the all-in carriage rate for bullion of 8s per cent (per £100), with two rates – 4s per cent on Gold, and 6s per cent on silver. The commanders of the transatlantic packets, paying these carriage costs out of their share of the freight money, were inclined to seek cheaper alternatives. This inclination caused an upset in the spring of 1811, when the bullion office at the Bank of England complained of delays in delivery. One complaint related to a delay in forwarding a consignment of dollars shipped in the packet **Lord Chesterfield** (3). Mr Russell having just raised his charges to 6s and 10s per cent, respectively, the packet owners too were naturally *desirous of sending it by a cheaper Conveyance.*

There were very few competitors in this trade, but a Mr Wynn, a local hotelier, coach proprietor, and PO contractor for mail distribution throughout West Cornwall, had for some years previously run a Falmouth – Exeter – London wagon trade as well. When another shipment of silver dollars landed out of the packet **Express**, was consigned to London via Wynn, Robert Russell wrote to Humble Thompson & Co the consignees, pointing out that:

... Captain Bullock on his arrival, (with the approbation of his Owner) delivered these Dollars to Mr. Wynn under the idea that he would make an abatement from the carriage, and gave him permission to forward them by any hired Carts, intimating that he might take his own time to convey them to London, as that was of no consequence to him. – had they been forwarded in this way I am satisfied from the quantity, they would not have been delivered in less than two months. – Mr. Wynn however delivered them to my Agent, as I had made an arrangement with him to send every thing by my wagons ...

Following these incidents the PO ordered that Russell & Co, were in future to convey all bullion freights to London. At the same time arrangements were made with the bullion office for the payment of the crown's share of freight direct to the PO in London. Hitherto the packet commanders, or owners, had received the freight money directly from the consignees, and had paid over the Crown's share to the packet agent at Falmouth. A practice which gave rise to complaints that there was *no public Check ... established as to the Accuracy & Amount of such Freight.* This process was now reversed, and thereafter the commanders and owners were paid their share of the freight by the packet agent – in arrears. On the 14th April 1812, Freeling noted with some satisfaction that the Bank of England were to ... *pay to this Department the Office share of Freights of Bullion amounting in the last Quarter to £1555 13s 7d.*

The carriage of bullion from the New World quickly exceeded all expectations, and in March 1832, following the loss of several 10-gun packet-brigs due to unknown causes, the Admiralty restricted the carriage of quicksilver (used in processing gold ores) to seven tons outwards, and bullion to 18 tons homeward – partially to spread the risk, and partially because they must have felt that these dense cargoes might in some measure have contributed to the loss of these packets.

By the mid-1830s, the flow of bullion from Mexico exceeded all previous levels. During 1831–32, 22 packets brought home nearly $9.1M, in coin and gold, from Tampico and Vera Cruz. Frequently bullion worth over a million dollars was left behind, and this sum does not include bullion freights carried by regular Royal Navy ships. Just a couple of year later, from an incomplete record for 11 out of 24 packet voyages during 1834–35, those 11 packets brought home nearly $6M, worth of bullion, valued at nearly £1.5M. A significant part of the trading wealth of Britain was brought home by the Falmouth packets.

11 *Free Trade & the Packet Mutiny*

Joining a packet

For a brief period the good order and discipline of the Falmouth Packet Service was disrupted in October 1810. Following yet another rummage by the customs officers, the crews of two packets refused to put to sea. This was deemed a mutiny, although the men offered neither threats nor violence against their officers. After a large and noisy gathering on shore, when the Riot Act was read, the packetmen dispersed peacefully. In less time than it took the news to reach London, the mutiny was all over, the packets had resumed their order of sailing, but the repercussions rumbled on.

As the situation began to unfold, a series of alarmist messages were sent to London by express riders. Days later these dribbled into the capital, fuelling a secondary fire long after the main conflagration had been extinguished. Ever fearful of a major civil uprising, hasty measures were set in motion by the central authorities, which, even though they had been appraised of the peaceful conclusion, they could not stop. Besides, they were convinced that drastic action was needed to – B*ring the Magistrates and People of Falmouth to a sense of their duty.* Measures were set in hand to apprehend the militant ringleaders; correct any errant commanders; and punish the townspeople. The underlying causes of discontent were as usual ignored.

On the morning of October 24th 1810, the packets **Duke of Marlborough** (2), and **Prince Adolphus**, were under immediate notice of sailing. Riding at the packet buoys in Carrick Roads, all hands had been mustered on board the night before. Topsails were set and sheeted home, with the packets trying impatiently at their moorings. Their passengers had embarked and the mails were on board. Both vessels were literally within minutes of slipping, *when they were boarded by the acting Tide-surveyor of His Majesty's Customs…* He, with a rummage crew, *broke open and took from the chests of the seamen … the little adventures contained therein.* Upset at being deprived of their little adventures, the seamen refused to put to sea. Such seizures had been made many times before but the situation was exacerbated by the decline in seamen's real wages due to rampant inflation during the Napoleonic wars. The cost of food was constantly increasing, and the packet seamen's basic wages of 28s per lunar month in the Lisbon service, and 31s 6d per month in the transatlantic services, were barely sufficient to supply their families *with the article of bread only.*

On August 15th 1810, a deputation composed of two men from each packet had presented the agent with a written request for an increase in wages, together with wage parity throughout the service, or the restoration of private venturing. Their case was presented calmly and respectfully and they were told it would receive full consideration.

The PO authorities, although warned of the high emotions at Falmouth, took their time in considering their response. The PMG were divided in their opinion. On the one hand they felt it was up to each commander how he divided his resources amongst his crew (a position greatly at odds with all previous establishment policy, custom and practice, where crew numbers and wages were predetermined, and commanders 'mulct' for sailing short handed). Yet, on the other hand they were not themselves averse to private trading, so long as the speed and defensive abilities of the packets were not jeopardised. They had reached no conclusions when the delegates returned to the agent's office at Bell's Court, on the 24th of August, but the disappointed men dispersed peacefully when told there was no news. Saverland, in order to prevent any increase in militancy, tried to hasten a decision, offering his opinion as to the reasonableness of the men's claim – to no avail.

Two months later, with matters still unresolved, the customs officers at Falmouth pounced. If they had done so on purpose they could not have chosen a more provocative moment to act. This seizure was the final straw – the men stopped work, and the packets were detained.

But, how had a situation arisen, in a Government controlled department, where an illicit form of income from petty private trading became so crucial to the economics of the service and the livelihood of the seamen and their families?

Throughout the history of the service, Treasury interference constantly tried to screw down operating costs. For all parties, this pressure found welcome relief in the form of an illegal subsidy – private trading. The favourable basic conditions were created back in Dummer's time – his contract allowing him five to ten tons of private cargo space per voyage, as a hedge against any losses on the carriage of the mail.

A few years down the line, with a persistent failure to address the problem, the bolder hands had assumed a right to trade on their own account. Others followed suit, and neither agents nor commanders seemed very interested in curtailing their activities. Indeed most took a large cut in the trade, and custom and practice became firmly established. At Falmouth, as throughout Cornwall, it was generally considered that free trade was fair trade.

Officially prohibited, the authorities constantly turned a blind eye to this trade as it enabled them to keep their seamen on a minimum wage. Soon everyone working in the packets had recourse to some degree of smuggling. The packets rarely came alongside the quays at Falmouth, normally riding at moorings off the town. All passengers, freight, and stores were conveyed to and from the packets in open boats, and the clandestine movement of goods at night was easily accomplished.

Free trade benefited a major part of the local community, and without it the economic situation in and around Falmouth would have been quite depressed. The commanders always claimed to have no knowledge of their crews' activities, but many were directly involved – how could they not be on board such small vessels!

After a brief flush of success for the customs authorities in 1743, matters settled down again, and private trading continued as normal. A little over forty years later there was another similar incident. The PO-owned packet **Greyhound** was seized at Jamaica in 1787, along with 47 cases of Dutch gin. This caused little reaction at Falmouth, as no private property was threatened. But when, in the following year, Captain Clarke of the **Queen Charlotte** (1), returned to Falmouth without his packet, matters took on a different hue. Having been seized and detained at Jamaica, again for smuggling cases of Hollands (gin), the **Queen Charlotte** (1) was liable to forfeiture. This threat, to this and other 'private' packets, drove the captains to precipitate action, which in turn caused a general disturbance:

> ... amongst the Packets folk, ... the Captains ... have Resolved that the Seamen shall not henceforth carry out any more than a Bushell of Potatoes each man, ... one Cheese to each mess ... nor their Chests for holding their Cloaths of a Greater Dimension than 3 feet in Length by 18 inches in Breadth and Depth in order to prevent them from purchasing abroad any kind of Goods which might subject the Ship to Forfeiture.

> In consequence of this resolve the Sailors (about 150), last Saturday (May 3rd) quitted the Packets, and sent the Agent here a Letter, Desiring more Wages in Lieu of the Priviledges of Carrying out Potatoes and Cheese for Sale on which traffick it seems they made Considerable Proffits. Alledging that most of them are married and have famylies to maintain, Chiefly Settled in this Town, for that they are not able to Support them at the Present Wages of 22 shillings per month, ...

Their wages had been set at twenty-three shillings per lunar month – less one shilling for the Chatham Chest – over twenty-five years earlier. All the active ingredients for unrest were present, and the circumstances were almost identical to those applying in 1743 and again in 1810.

Captains Bull and Clarke set off post haste to London, to explain the situation to the PO officials, while the men regularly petitioned for higher wages. Within a few days they were advised that *... the Postmasters are Inclined to Redress their Complaints by Ordering an Addition to their Wages...* On which assurance most of the crews returned to their duties – even though captains D'Auvergne and Richards, of the PO packets **Speedy** (1) and **Roebuck**, had dashed precipitously off to

Plymouth and obtained replacement crews. Fortunately this provocative action did not aggravate matters further and the sailors … *conducted themselves very soberly and peacefully.*

While matters seemed to have been resolved, the PO was, as ever, slow to act. Two months later, even though nothing had been done about raising the crews' wages, the commanders ordered a further reduction in the size of the men's chests, and that *no cheese and potatoes* at all were to be embarked. The men refused to join their ships and feelings ran high in Falmouth. When some of the commanders were insulted in the streets, they tried to invoke martial law, but the Corporation persuaded them to be satisfied with the appointment of additional special constables. Eventually the postal authorities confirmed their intention that the men's wages should be raised, and they returned to work. But still the PO was in no hurry, and it doesn't appear that the wages were actually increased until 1790/91, when they were raised to twenty-eight shillings as part of the general reforms.

Eventually the service settled down again, and in a short time private trading was resumed – everything continued as normal. Even after the far-reaching service reforms of the 1790s, private adventuring continued almost unabated. In July 1795, shortly after one of those periodic resumptions of the Corunna packet service, the PMG minuted:

> *Great and frequent complaints are made by the Court of Spain on account of the smuggling carried on by the Corunna Packets. Let Mr. Pender inform the Captains in the most peremptory manner that if these Complaints are continued, & discovered to be well founded, the captain who shall have been guilty of suffering any Contraband or illegal Trade, will infallibly be dismissed.*

As there were only two packets employed on the Corunna service, there was little room for speculation – it had to be either the **Duchess of York**, (Jones), or the **Princess of Brunswick**, (Blight). However, these packets were augmented from time to time by Spanish packets, and the diplomatic complaint leading to the above minute may have been a 'tit for tat' reprisal. Early in 1795 the Spanish packet **Grimaldi**, when forced into Penzance by heavy weather, was found to be carrying two contraband bales of indigo. It was a clear breach of the reciprocal agreement covering these packets, but the Customs officials at Penzance were ordered to release the **Grimaldi**, *on the payment of the duty and a Satisfaction to the Seizing Officer*, in lieu of his seizure reward.

Another minor disturbance occurred in 1801, and although less well documented, it may have arisen from a seizure made by the Tide-Surveyor, Mr Whitter, on September 7th 1801, when he … *seized on board the* **Earl Leicester** (2) *Packet, Samuel Steele Master for Jamaica, some Potatoes, Cheese, Beef & Butter for being illegally shipped for exportation* …

When later questioned as to the exact nature of the goods

seized, and the commander's roll in events, Whitter replied that:

> The four Casks of Beef & Tongues in particular were shipped on board as Merchandise, the Captain having received a Sum of Money for the Freight of them. I have also to acquaint you that the Corks, Pickles, Shoes and Pins, were seized by me for being shipt on board the said Packet with the intention of being illegally exported out of this Kingdom, without having obtained the licence of the Honble Board for that purpose.

The final consequences of this specific incident are not known, the packet continued in the service. Such incidents certainly added to the tension at Falmouth, and it was about this time that the PO appointed a local packet Inspector & Searcher, to try and prevent private trading. A further clamp down on 'private trade' was reported in the *Cornwall Gazette* of Saturday, July 17th 1802:

> An order has been received here ... to put a stop to the exportation of goods of every kind by the packets. It is well known that the trade ... has long been carried on with the knowledge of Government, who derived great advantage from it; as articles of English manufacture ... exported ... could not claim the drawback. ... whatever be the cause of this order, the consequence will be fatal to Falmouth. Manchester and other goods to a very large amount have already been seized by the officers of the Customs. ... – it was the last stake the war had left us.

But the trade and attempts to suppress it continued (see petition 1806 p136).

Compared with the normal seizures of brandy, Geneva (gin), rum, tobacco and tea, which featured in Cornish custom house sales of this era, the variety of foreign goods on offer at Falmouth sales, suggests that many of these items were seized out of the packets, although they were never reported as such in the adverts. This suggestion is borne out by another advert published in the *Royal Cornwall Gazette*, of August 8th 1807.

Capt Lovell Todd's packet **Prince of Wales** (2), having been captured on her return passage from Lisbon, was later retaken by HMS **Poulette**, Capt James Dunbar, and brought into Falmouth on September 1st 1805. The packet appears to have been restored, but her cargo was impounded pending judgement of the High Court of Admiralty. Nearly two years later a Commission of Appraisement and Sale was issued by that court, resulting in a long list of items of foreign manufacture being advertised for sale.

Which brings us back to the events of October 24th 1810. After rifling the **Prince Adolphus**, the customs' rummage crew moved on to the **Duke of Marlborough** (2). The packet agent was summoned on board the former vessel, but nothing Saverland could say changed the crew's minds. Even the threat of dismissal from the service, with the resulting loss of their press protections, failed to move the men to return to their duties.

Getting nowhere, Saverland called on the assistance of the local naval receiving officer, and later that morning Captain Slade boarded the **Prince Adolphus**, with a naval press gang from HMS **Experiment**. Full of righteous zeal Captain Slade immediately set about the recalcitrant seamen – though as he later reported, his men were not at first fully behind him:

> Had I not Sir at the most eminent risk of my Life secured the Crews of the two Packets who mutinied, with only seven Men, all of whom I believe belonged to this Neighbourhood, and even to induce them to act I was obliged to draw my Sword and threaten to run them through the Body, had I not exposed and exerted myself, there is every reason to believe not one of the Mutineers would have been apprehended as a punishment for their highly criminal conduct, and as an example to deter others in future from a repetition of the like on any imaginary or real Grievance.

To show just how out of keeping this behaviour was, less than ten days earlier the **Duke of Marlborough** (2) had returned home from Lisbon. A few miles off Falmouth, during the morning of her subsequent arrival, she was attacked by a 14-gun French privateer. This attack brought forth Capt Bull's singular call to arms, when – no doubt while brandishing his sword – he declaimed: Men – there is Pendennis Castle; there is your home and your families are watching you. So fight! And fight they did, holding a close engagement for well over an hour. It was touch and go, even to the point where Capt Bull ordered the mails to be cut away and sunk. But, just as the Frenchmen were about to board, a discharge of 'canister' from one of the packet's guns cleared the privateer's forecastle and she sheered off and withdrew.

> The engagement was seen from the heights near Falmouth, where the friends of Captain John Bull, whose name is truly characteristic of his spirit, and his gallant little band beheld the unequal contest and glorious triumph of these heroes with indescribable sensations.

During this engagement, four of the packet's crew were wounded, but fortunately none were killed. The PMG was so pleased, that Capt Bull and his crew were later awarded four month's pay and smart money – amounting to £310 8s. This then was packetmen's normal behaviour, but their world was soon turned on its ears. One minute they were feted heroes, and the next outcast mutineers! Almost before they knew it twenty-six seamen from the two packets' crews had been seized and impressed, and sent on board HMS **Experiment**.

By virtue of a Commission of Appraisement and Sale, issued out of the High Court of Admiralty, of the United Kingdom, addressed to Laz. Hingston, and Robt. Crowgey, merchants, Falmouth,

WILL BE SOLD BY AUCTION,

On THURSDAY the 3d day of September next, by ten o'clock in the forenoon, at the SHIP and CASTLE Tavern, Falmouth,

THE under-mentioned GOODS, recaptured in the Prince of Wales Packet, Capt. Lovell Todd, on her passage from Lisbon to Falmouth, by his Majesty's ship Poulette, Capt. James Dunbar:

    145 Pieces plain and striped Muslins
     73 Ditto, plain and coloured Tambour ditto
     98 Ditto, Book ditto
      5 Pieces of Tambour laced Cambric
      4 Ditto Lappet Ditto
    148 Doz. & 2 Clouded Border Muslin Shawls
     52 Doz. & 3 Printed Border ditto
    19½ Ditto, Lappet ditto
    417 Doz & 7 Colored Border Muslin Handkerchiefs
     39 Dozen Book ditto
    119 Dozen Lappet Book Ditto
     27 Doz. & 10 Tambour Ditto
     39 Ditto, Madras Ditto
    273 Doz. & 4 Pullicat Ditto
      9 Doz. & 3 Plain and laced Cambric Ditto
      4 Doz. & 6 Tambour Ditto
    120 Doz. & 9 Men and Women's Cotton Hose
     23 Pieces of Printed Cotton
     14 Pieces of Furniture Ditto
     24 Pieces of Plain Calico
     27 Pieces of Quilting
     12 Pieces of Dimity
     58 Pieces of Velveteen
     22 Pieces of Velveret
      1 Piece of Sattinet
      1 Piece of Scarlet Velvet Plush
     15 Dozen Cotton Breeches Pieces
     20 Grose of Gilt and Plated Coat Buttons
         And sundry other Articles.

The Goods may be viewed, Catalogues had, and further particulars known, by applying to

LAZ. HINGSTON,   } Commissioners
AND
ROBT. CROWGEY,   }

Falmouth, July 23, 1807.

*This lengthy Salvage Sale advert, published after the recapture of the packet **Prince of Wales**, by HMS **Poulette**, gives an idea of the wide range of merchandise smuggled by the packetmen. The listed items were the property of the crew, and were traded to supplement their wages (The Cornwall Centre)*

As word spread, the crews of the nine other packets in harbour quit their ships. The following day they assembled in front of the agent's office, seeking the liberation of their mates confined on board the **Experiment**. Now, the 25th also happened to be a public holiday – the 50th Jubilee of King George III – and Saverland was alarmed at the number of angry seamen assembled, backed by a very vocal crowd of inhabitants. He sent for the mayor, who soon arrived with fellow magistrates and members of the corporation. They deemed it expedient to read the Riot Act, but this did not please Capt Slade, RN, who had requested:

> ... the Magistrates to take measures for their being surrounded, in order that the Ring Leaders might be picked out ... in spite of all I could say to the contrary, the Riot Act was read, and the Mutineers allowed to disperse.

For the Falmouth officials, the reading of the Riot Act had the desired effect. The crowd dispersed, and the religious ceremonies and Jubilee celebrations continued with only the slightest interruption. At one p.m., HM Schooner **Mullet**, and the other naval vessels, fired a Royal Salute, but if there was any reaction to this cannonade it was not recorded. The packet seamen departed 'mostly into the country', where they kept well away from marauding press gangs from the **Experiment**.

Later that day the **Duke of Marlborough** (2) sailed with the Lisbon mail – her thirteen impressed crew members being replaced by naval seamen from the **Experiment**. However, there were insufficient naval hands available to man the **Prince Adolphus** as well. Her mail for Malta was forwarded later that day by HM Cutter **Dart**, which had previously been appointed to take the mail for Cadiz. Several days later 27th or 29th (reports differ) Capt Rogers took the **Countess of Chichester** out with the Leeward Islands mails, while HM Ketch **Gleaner**, hastily procured in lieu of the distressed naval schooner **Mullet**, took out the Surinam mails, and HM Cutter **Britannia** took out the next Lisbon and Cadiz mails. At most the mails were delayed by only four days.

While the mutiny was now a non-event, there was no reprieve for most of the men pressed from the two packets. One – John Brewer – was fortunate enough to be released, but on 12th November the remaining twenty-five were put on HM Brig **Mariner** for passage to Sir Charles Cotton's fleet in the Mediterranean. At Falmouth, under an apparently calm surface there was deep local animosity and some hotheads began circulating flammatory notices, aimed at the customs men. One found in the street outside the Shipwright's Arms, declaring:

> Head Quarters   Bicken Hill
> Sir – please to post this
> There is 150 Guineas for any Men or Man that will murder Platt, Pope or Clift, as we are determined to do it, as the(y) have ruined we and our families if we can't get that done, we will blow up the Watch House one Night.
> Signed Victory or Death

No 2 Bell's Court Reputedly the Falmouth Packet Office and the scene of the reading of the Riot Act during the Packet Mutiny of October 1810. Home of the late Cornwall Maritime Museum (now incorporated in the National Maritime Museum Cornwall) it originally had a view of the street through a handsome iron gate... but later became somewhat isolated behind new buildings in Market Street

Platt, Pope and Clift, were the tidesmen whose seizures had sparked of the mutiny. Attention was later turned on Samuel Pellew, the Collector of Customs:

Falmouth Oct.r 31. 1810

Sir,   I have to inform you that I am one of a party sworn to destroy you & two others, but on reflection, in gratitude for past favours received at your hands, induces me to give you this caution.

The manner the Packetmen has been plunder'd and with a shameless show of Religion & Justice is beyond all example and calls aloud for vengeance In vain may you throw the odium on your Boatmen, they are comparatively innocent – with your atrocities your die is cast. I tremble for the consequences – You I wish to quit the Town directly and leave the others to their inevitable fate. To meet their hypocritical deserts – you have just God to call on, and beg you will not waste the time you have yet left, to bewail it to eternity – if Pills can not be properly applied, a more subtle mode will be taken,

beware & secret

your Fr.

Whatever the past services, the law of the land, and/or the rights and wrongs of their case, Pellew's 'friend', and his mates sincerely believed in the justice of their cause.

The two men deputed to carry the packetmen's message to London were, Richard Pascoe and John Parker. As neither was then a serving packetman they could not be classed at mutineers, but they were singled out by Freeling for special treatment. On arrival they were given over to the City Marshall, and jailed on the Lord Mayor's instructions pending examination. The Lord Mayor having exceeded his authority, they were both released a few days later, and immediately began an action against Freeling for false arrest. This action could have become embittered and protracted, but matters being now settled in Falmouth, Pascoe and Parker were persuaded not to press charges.

A meeting of the senior burgesses of Falmouth on the 29th of October, induced the packet agent to issue a public notice declaring a general amnesty, and with Freeling's approval the amnesty was extended to all:

> ... *with the exception of the undermentioned Persons who cannot on any account be admitted into the Service of their Lordships ..., namely:*
>
> | | | |
> |---|---|---|
> | Ezekiel Williams | William Roundtree | Joseph Cane |
> | William Blackwell | George Wells | John Parker. |

Why not Pascoe as well, who can tell? But, despite these 'blackings', the men accepted the offer, and by Friday November 2nd all were duly mustered on board their packets.

Between the 1st and 4th of November, another three mails left Falmouth by the regular packets – **Princess Augusta** (3) for the Leeward Islands; **Prince of Wales** (2) for Lisbon; and the **Prince Adolphus** for Jamaica. Unfortunately, this return to normality was too late to stay the heavy hand of authority.

On the 2nd of November, Saverland received orders to immediately transfer the service to Plymouth, and on the 5th and 6th the eight remaining packets at Falmouth were marshalled under the guns of HM Ships **Niemen**, **North Star** and **Hawke**, and escorted to Plymouth. Here hasty arrangements were made, but the widespread nature of the anchorage, and the natural priority given to HM warships, did little to enhance the packet service. Staff from Falmouth had to be sent up and accommodated in inns and hotels, and a temporary office found.

In the event Plymouth failed to live up to its longstanding claim to be a better packet port than Falmouth. There had been no time to lay packet-mooring buoys, even if a suitable spot could have been found. The navy had no spare berths, so the packets had to anchor wherever they could. For one reason or another nearly every packet that sailed from Plymouth over the next few months was 'forced' into Falmouth, before she could proceed on her voyage. Those at sea when the mutiny occurred, returned to Falmouth, only to be told they had to go on to Plymouth, which delayed their turn-round. The dockyard facilities at Plymouth were over-stretched with naval work, so any damaged packets had to return to Falmouth to effect repairs. By the 13th Saverland reported:

> I hope the packets do not remain here as a fixed station. If they do, the establishment must be greatly increased and the correspondence delayed. Both the West India and the American mails were ready, yesterday, by about noon; but, what with the passengers in different and distant inns, the Packets in different places, the cartage of the mails, the purchasing of their anchors in very deep water, pilotage – not one man-of-war goes to sea without, so dangerous is the passage – is such that I see we shall not gain anything in getting to sea, though the mail arrives here in the morning.

The two mails referred to were taken out by the packets **Express** and **Adventure**, neither of which sailed for a full twenty-four hours after the mails had arrived at Plymouth, and both were forced into Falmouth by bad weather on their way down Channel.

Meanwhile the **Diana** had parted her cable during one of a succession of gales then sweeping across the West of England, and was nearly driven ashore. The **Dispatch** was nearly run foul of by HMS **Stately**, which only just missed her, hitting a hulk instead. The **Princess Elizabeth** (2) snagged a brand new anchor cable costing £140, cutting it in two.

CUSTOM-HOUSE, LONDON,
December, 1812.

WHEREAS it has been represented to the Commissioners of His Majesty's Customs that a threatening Letter was on the 28th ult. received by Joseph Platt, an Officer of the Customs, at the Port of Falmouth, of which the following is a Copy:

" Pray to God to forgive you.

" JOSEPH PLATT, your doom is fixed as Per-
" ceval, received his Death by a Ball so you
" shall fall."

" Your late proceedings with the Packets;
" has driven me to Despair, & ere I leave this
" Earth, my determination is fixed to put End
" to your wicked and cruel Existance, unless
" you discontinue your committing such Rob-
" beries as you & your Crew has perpetrated for
" this some time past, I give you, J. Platt to
" consider of this as above until 30th March
" 1813, my Dr Friend although my cruel Ene-
" mie, and my Ruin, for the sake of your Soul,
" pray to Jesus to forgive you, I say again your
" Fate is fixed."

" A Frend to the"
Community."

" Falmouth, 28th Novr. 1812.

The said Commissioners of His Majesty's Customs in order to bring to Justice the Person who wrote or sent the said Letter, are hereby pleased to offer a REWARD of FIFTY POUNDS to any Person or Persons who shall discover and apprehend, or cause to be discovered and apprehended the Person or Persons who wrote or sent the said Letter, or caused the same to be written and sent, to be paid by the Collector of His Majesty's Customs at the Port of Falmouth, upon conviction.

By Order of the Commissioners,
H. RICHMOND, Secretary.

*Custom House Reward, 1812
The packetmen might have been back at work, but the customs officers were neither forgiven nor forgotten. Nearly two years after the 'mutiny' there was still an undercurrent of unrest, and rumbling disquiet in Falmouth (The Cornwall Centre)*

A week later Saverland again wrote, advising that T*he Packets lie very badly here. Unless moorings are laid down, and a separate place assigned, some of them will be lost before the winter is over.* He was not exaggerating. Plymouth Sound was then an open anchorage. On Sunday December 16th, the **Prince Ernest** packet, bound for Jamaica, drove ashore under the Mount Edgcumbe Battery. She was fortunately got off without much damage, but the risk of total loss had been all too real.

Christopher Saverland Post Office Packet Agent at Falmouth between 1810 and 1823, this portrait depicts him as a strong forthright character. He needed to be, and while his authority was severely tested by the Packet Mutiny of 1810, he came through and proved himself a great asset to the service

By early February even the PMG were ready to admit that the move to Plymouth was a mistake – but they had taught Falmouth a lesson. The return took some time to arrange, but as T*he* B*ristol* M*irror*, of Saturday, February 9th, 1811 reported. It was:

> … *impossible to depict the general joy at Falmouth, on account of the order for the return of the Packets. On the news reaching that place several hogsheads of beer were given away to the populace; some brilliant displays of fire-works took place, and bonfires blazed in every direction.*

Between the 13th and 15th of February all the thirteen packets then at Plymouth returned to Falmouth. If anything, their return caused even greater disruption to the service than the mutiny itself. But eventually things soon returned to normal – continuing just as they had before!

12 Peace: Admiralty Packets & Experiments in Steam

News that the Admiralty was about to take over the management of the Falmouth Packet Service, hit Falmouth like a bombshell in the latter part of 1822. Since the unhappy events of the autumn of 1810, Falmouth and the packet service had felt reasonably secure from any undue interest of the Royal Navy. A take-over, while hinted at occasionally, had never seemed a realistic proposition. But now wild rumours circulated that hundreds of seamen were to be thrown out of work, packet proprietors to be rendered bankrupt, and even the old hoary chestnut of operations being transferred to Plymouth, lock stock and barrel. For some months great anxiety was felt throughout the district.

Steam packet **Echo**

The proposed transfer of authority was promoted by Lord Melville (First Lord of the Admiralty, 1812–27), possibly at the suggestion of Capt King, RN – who was to become the first Naval Superintendent of Packets. Melville had previously raised the possibility in 1814, when he considered that packet losses were suspiciously high. He thought this resulted from some collusion with the enemy, or insurance swindle. The RN having been called upon to provide a number of small vessels to support the mail service, from time to time, Melville also believed the Admiralty could run it more efficiently and more effectively. However, the PO was in no mood to

Falmouth Custom House Headquarters of the customs service at Falmouth at the time of the Packet Mutiny, its austere and slightly forbidding façade was designed to instil a measure of respect and awe amongst wayward seafarers

relinquish control at that time. After the war Melville was bombarded with letters from half-pay officers seeking employment, and with the reduced size of the peacetime navy he saw this as an opportunity to form an effective naval reserve. The Government of the day were convinced by his arguments, especially by Melville's assertion that with naval efficiency the number of packets would be quickly reduced from 30 to 26.

The worst fears of the packet commanders and owners, as well as the people of Falmouth in general, were not realised. Concessions were made, and on April 6th 1823 the transfer to Admiralty control took effect. No contract packets nor packetmen were immediately laid off as a result, but as individual contracts expired they were generally not renewed. Civil packets and seamen were gradually released, to be replaced by Admiralty 10-gun brigs, manned by naval crews.

The **Astraea**, a cut-down frigate, was stationed at Falmouth as a depôt ship, with Capt William King, RN nominally in command, as the Superintendent of Packet operations at Falmouth.

On the effective day 28 civil packets were transferred to Admiralty control. One new civil packet was nearing completion at Falmouth, but there were no Admiralty packets ready for service. The 10-gun brig **Frolic** was still being converted at Devonport, *by the reduction of her masts, yards, etc.* Commissioned under Lieutenant TC Barron on April 28th, it was the June 20th before she was ready to set out on her proving voyage to Lisbon. Previously, Barron had commanded the civil packet **Prince Ernest** (from December 1820), but she was stranded in a gale near Gibraltar on the 2nd February 1823, and became a total loss. Fortunately no lives were lost and Lt Barron's services were retained. However, on only her second voyage as a packet, en route for Halifax, Lt Barron had the misfortune to run the **Frolic** onto Sable Island. After throwing her guns and stores overboard, he got her off and arrived at Halifax on the 21st September. Again Lt Barron was allowed to retain the command of his vessel, and he and the **Frolic** continued in the service for several years.

Meanwhile, the last civil packet to enter the service had been completed, and was launched as the **Lord Melville** at Falmouth on the 20th September, having been:

> Christened by the lady of Captain King, Admiralty Superintendent of Packets at Falmouth. The **Lord Melville** is one of the larger class of packets, and is better adapted for defence, than many of the smaller class employed during the war.

Initially commanded by Capt Furze, and later by Lt Charles Webbe, RN, she was a fine packet, but after sixteen years' service she was lost without trace, after sailing from Falmouth for Halifax, on October 5th 1839.

During the autumn of 1823 two civil packets closed their PO careers. James Porteous' **Lady Arabella** returned from her last voyage on October 9th, when he left Falmouth to supervise the final fitting out of HM Brig **Magnet** (one of the few RN packet-brigs to have a civil commander). Shortly afterwards the **Blucher** (ex-**Little Catherine**), a PO owned vessel which had served as a reserve packet for commanders while building replacements, was advertised for sale, returning to civilian ownership under her former name in the following March.

During this same period, HM Brigs **Eclipse**, **Lyra**, **Partridge**, **Emulous** and **Magnet** followed the **Frolic** into the service, but the demands on these vessels proved much more onerous than the Admiralty had anticipated. The introduction of Admiralty packet brigs was not countered by the release of civil packets. The service grew instead of shrinking, and by February–March 1827 there were 41 packets in use – 18 civil and 23 HM. It was not entirely their fault, a number of additional service routes had been added, but the Admiralty had misunderstood efficiency to mean running a regular, *damned fine copper bottomed service*, while the PO understood that it meant running an economic service to schedule. Intentionally or not, the Admiralty also tended to hide their true operational costs by constantly moving vessels into and out of the service.

During 1824 the Admiralty extended the Brazilian service from Rio de Janeiro down to Monte Video and Buenos Ayres. Pioneered by the **Countess of Chichester** between February and July, this formed a separate route, requiring six or seven extra packets. The old route serving Rio, Bahia, and Pernambuco and the new route serving Rio, Monte Video and Buenos Ayres. On both routes, depending on the season, the prevailing winds caused the running order of the ports of call to be reversed – six months one way and six the other. These were the longest routes in the service, with round voyages averaging about 160 days. In consequence these were the last routes to be privatised, when taken over by commercial steamer services at the end of 1850.

The main Jamaica service was extended in 1825, to include, Carthagena, and at the end of 1826, a new service was provided, via Jamaica to Vera Cruz and Tampico, and back to Falmouth via Havana. Proved by the **Lady Mary Pelham** (2) during October–January 1826–27, the Mexico service proved a good earner in terms of bullion carried from the Mexican treasury and consignments of mercury shipped to Mexico for processing the gold ores.

Under Admiralty control there was some reduction in round voyage times, but these were mostly achieved by cutting the time spent at the different ports of call. In a further attempt to improve the speed and regularity of the Falmouth packet service the Admiralty introduced steam-vessels into the overseas packet service in the early

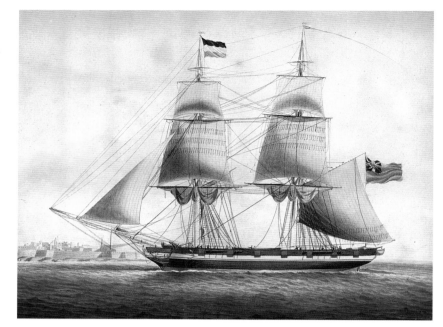

*The **Lady Mary Pelham**, 1816–35 Another of the Cammillieri packet portraits. The second packet of this name, she is depicted at Malta in 1818, under the command of Capt James Hay (NMMC)*

1830s. Used very much as working test-beds, here the Admiralty gained their first practical experience of working steam vessels in regular service.

Their first paddle-steamer venture in this service was a proving trial carried out by HM Steam Vessel **Meteor**, under the command of Lt Symons RN. Of 296 tons (displacement), and powered by two 50-horse power engines, during February and March 1830 she made a round voyage from Falmouth to Corfu and back, calling at Gibraltar, Malta , Zante and Patrass each way. The round voyage was completed in 47 days and set the new standard for this route, as against the previous norm of 90 plus days for the sailing packets. While the **Meteor's** proving voyage was being evaluated, the sailing packet **Osborne** took out the March Mediterranean mails, but thereafter this route became the exclusive domain of HM steam vessels. **Meteor**, **Echo** and a succession of others maintaining the service until it was privatised seven years later.

With the paddle steamers averaging 47–48 days for the round voyage, three steam vessels should have been able to maintain the monthly service schedule – but in practice they could not. Heavy mechanical wear, coupled with frequent boiler breakdowns, meant that eight different steam vessels were needed to maintain the service during the first two years. The majority of Admiralty steam-vessels then in use had been built in the Admiralty dockyards. Intended as Cherokee class sailing brigs, they were eventually completed as paddle steamers. As Lieutenant's commands, they were rated as 'sloops' and were designated HM Steam Vessels (HMSt V). In addition to those built in the Admiralty dockyards, two other steamers built in private yards for commercial service, were bought in to bolster the service – HMStV **Messenger** and **Hermes**. Although there were many service complaints about their light scantlings, between 1830 and 1832, these two vessels completed as many, if not more, voyages than any other steam vessel in the service.

Three factors governed the length of voyage that could be undertaken by these early paddle steamers under power – their coal consumption (a product of engine and boiler efficiency), the amount of bunker coal that they could stow, and the distance between replenishment stocks of steam coal. Although provisional stocks of bunker coal had been provided for the **Meteor's** proving voyage, it was quickly apparent that permanent coal depôts needed to be established at strategic points along the route. From July 1830, the Navy Board regularly advertised in the London Gazette, seeking tenders for the phased delivery of steam coal to Gibraltar and Malta, and a key measure of the global expansion of RN steam ships, was the progressive establishment of a network of coaling depôts across the oceans of the world.

These first steam packets were desperately inefficient, consuming prodigious quantities of coal to generate steam at four to five pounds per square inch (ppsi.). Rather perversely they relied on the vacuum stroke (developing around 18 to 20 ppsi.), for most of their power. The 'steam stroke' just repriming the cylinder for the next cycle. Propelled by paddle wheels, the motive force was provided by a pair of side level steam engines supplied with steam from two or three 'haystack' boilers. Most naval officers of the day had little mechanical understanding, and little inclination to learn about dirty engines. The engineers were not officers, indeed, many were civilians provided by the engine manufacturers. As far as many deck officers were concerned the sign of an efficient and attentive engine-room staff was plenty of smoke billowing from the funnel, and steam constantly blowing off from the safety valve.

On only her fourth Mediterranean voyage, the **Meteor** suffered a major boiler failure when off the coast of North Africa. Later during that same voyage she ran out of coal when thwarted by head winds off the coast of Portugal. Forced into the Spanish port of Vigo to re-bunker, the coal taken on was insufficient to get her home. After having burnt ... *every spare spar, bulkhead, topmast, water-cask, and every thing they could find,* they were ignominiously forced to anchor seven miles short of Falmouth while more coal was ferried out to them. She eventually reached Falmouth on June 30th 1831, with thirteen passengers on board, and eight days behind schedule. Her commander's subsequent report of defects was significant – the final part (in bold type) covering the replacement of the ships fixtures and fittings burnt in attempting to maintain steam:

Defects of H M *Steam Vessel* Meteor, *Lt Symons, Commander – 30th June 1831.*

New Brasses for Centre of Beams wanting

New Brasses for Side Rods and Ends of Beams

Boilers want repairing, having given way in several places, owing to their having worn thin, and the Stay Bolts constantly breaking.

Hot Water Pumps defective

Threads of Bolts and Plumbing Blocks stripped

Pistons defective

Paddle Wheels want repairing

Boss of the Wheel defective

New Glans (Glands) for different Pumps wanting

Hold down Bolts of framing of the Engines want examining

Several new Keys for Engine wanted

New Crank Pin for Larboard Engine wanted

Decks want Caulking

Illuminators leak

Sponsing (paddle sponsons) wants repair

Ladders want repairing

Boats want repair

Glass wants replacing

Pantries want repairing

Bulwarks great part gone

Bedplaces

Tables

Stools.

(Signed) W H *Symons*   *Lieutenant & Commander*

The unseasonal north-easterly winds persisted, and the following month HMStV **Confiance** also ran out of fuel, this time just off the Isles of Scilly. Having *burnt all her spare woodwork*, a Cowes pilot cutter, hovering off the islands, brought in the mails and news of her predicament. The sailing packet **Magnet**, then at Falmouth between voyages, was quickly loaded with coal and sent off to relieve the steamer. A couple of days later, with the **Confiance** once more under her own power, the crew of the **Magnet** were able to enjoy the luxury of a tow home.

As Lt Symons' report shows, the moving parts of these early steam vessels were subject to very heavy wear, and as well as consuming prodigious quantities of coal they were extremely prone to mechanical breakdowns:

H M *steamer* **Columbia**, *Lt Ede, sailed from Falmouth on the 20th inst. (Mon.) with the mail for Portugal. After being at sea for two days, the crank of one of her engines broke, and she was unable to proceed farther (sic) on her voyage. She remained in this state two days, when they fell in with a pilot boat, which landed a passenger at Mount's Bay, who brought intelligence of the accident to Capt. King, Naval Superintendent at Falmouth, on Sunday the 26th, when the* **African** *and* **Flamer** *steamers were dispatched in search of her. The* **Columbia** *continued to work up as far as the Lizard, when she was towed in by the* **Confiance**. *The two steamers which were sent in search of the* **Columbia** *missed her in the night. The* **Confiance** *sailed next day with* **Columbia's** *mails, at which time the other steamers had not arrived, and the passenger who had volunteered his services to come on shore in the pilot boat, and who had gone out in the* **African** *in expectation of falling in with the* **Columbia**, *was left behind – he was charged with very important dispatches.*

Western Luminary – Tuesday June 4th 1833

In 1830, after only two voyages as a packet, HMStV **Echo** was withdrawn to test Cornish tubular boilers at sea, with high pressure steam – 15 ppsi. – and expansive working. Due to prejudice and mismanagement, the trials conducted during 1831–2 proved inconclusive and set back British marine steam development by ten years. When removed from the **Echo** in November 1833, these boilers were as good as new – unlike most marine boilers of the day, which had a very short life span. Having previously condemned them, it is intriguing to find that John Kingston took the trouble to produce a detailed coloured sketch of them when removed!

While steam vessels proved effective on the Mediterranean service, they were unable (as planned) to absorb the Lisbon service into their Mediterranean schedule, and they did not at first have the coal capacity/efficiency to undertake any of the transatlantic routes. These routes remained the domain of the sailing packets for the time being, but already the North Atlantic service to the United States had been effectively hijacked by commercial shipping lines operating between New York and Liverpool. New York was dropped as a terminal packet port towards the end on 1826, and Lt Baron's **Frolic** appears to have been the last packet to call there before returning to Falmouth on February 26th 1827. Thereafter the North American packets provided a service between Falmouth and Bermuda, via Halifax, with a local feeder service running between Halifax and New York. As the 1830s unwound the contracts for the civil packet expired, and one by one they were retired from the service until the **Camden**, was sold out to London owners in October 1838, and the **Lord Melville** was lost in October/November 1839.

Two aspects of the old service that were not totally eliminated by Admiralty control were smuggling and private trading. An element of smuggling, though on a petty scale, continued to be carried on by the lower ranks – principally in tobacco. The new steam vessels were particularly suspect.

> *On the arrival of the* **Messenger** *steam packet Lieut. Aplin, at Falmouth on Saturday last (21/1/1832), from the Mediterranean, she was immediately boarded by three custom house officers from London, who it is supposed received information from a discharged engineer, that smuggled goods were on board. They proceeded to search in places of concealment of which they appeared to be well informed, and discovered a quantity of tobacco, &c. which they seized and deposited in the Custom-house.*

As indicated, this seizure was the result of a detailed statement from a disgruntled informant – one well acquainted with the layout of the engine-room! Their search revealed

414 lbs. leaf tobacco, and	
44 lbs. cigars –	*under the planking of the coal hole;*
60 lbs. cigars –	*under the plates of the engine-room;*
15 lbs. cigars –	*under the cinders in the smith's forge on deck;*
2½ lbs. cigars –	*in the starboard paddle-box;*
2 ¼ lbs. cigars –	*under the sails in the sail-room;*
16 lbs. leaf tobacco –	*under firewood in the fore-hold;*
12 glass tumblers –	*under a false sill in the engine-room*

According to the rummage crew:

> *The officers gave us every assistance, with the exception of the boatswain, who, with the engineers, stokers, and coal-trimmers, acted in a very insubordinate manner, and threw every impediment in our way.*

Private trading, now essentially an officers' privilege, was formally acknowledged by the introduction of a special customs declaration form. It was mainly confined to small quantities of wines and spirits, though some of the surviving forms show that small commercial parcels were also being carried.

Unfortunately the Admiralty 10-gun brigs did not prove very satisfactory packets. Deep waisted and low decked, if they shipped a heavy sea, their small freeing ports and massive bulwarks retained a vast quantity of free water on the upper deck, causing dangerous instability. There was also considerable pressure put upon the naval commanders to improve performance. Consequently many were very hard pressed, and all too many left Falmouth never to be heard of again. During the first decade of Admiralty control eight or nine of these vessels were tragically lost. Most disappeared without trace, taking all hands, passengers, mail and bullion with them. Although cut down from their original heavy service rigs, their crews were also reduced in an attempt to contain operating costs and they were still 'heavily hatted'.

As losses mounted, these packets were dubbed 'coffin brigs'.

And, while opinions differed widely as to the underlying cause, popular blame fell on the design of the 10-gun brigs, and their low freeboard. Most were lost beating to westward against the Atlantic seas. A few made it home with harrowing tales of close escapes. HM Brig **Kingfisher**, under Lt Poore, arrived at Falmouth, from Vera Cruz, on January 30th 1828 having *sailed from that place 16th ult.; and the Havannah, the 28th ditto; with loss of boats, guns thrown overboard, &c, having experienced very severe weather* – an all too common litany. (see List of Packet Losses under Admiralty Control pp132/133))

The criticism of the 10-gun brigs' hull design was never officially accepted by the Admiralty, but they were eventually forced to take action in 1834, announcing that four new brigs of a new class were to be built. The first commissioned as a packet was the 358-ton **Pandora**, built on Capt Symonds' principle, but some were diverted to other duties on completion. **Pandora** bore an *excellent character as a sea-boat, either lying-too, running, or on a wind*. And her accommodation was considered *very superior*. Having *three large cabins, with various state-rooms, is six feet between decks, and carries 23 tons of water and five months provisions under hatches*. Unfortunately she was hastily completed, and later suffered from an early onset of extensive rot.

Other packets of the **Pandora** class followed, but the new class was not problem-free. The **Star** sailed on her maiden voyage to Halifax on November 7th 1835, and was nearly overwhelmed beating into the teeth of an Atlantic gale. Seventeen days out of Falmouth:

> At two o'clock on the morning of the 24th a heavy sea struck the ship on the
> starboard beam, throwing her on her beam ends, and stove in all our sky and
> dead lights, washed overboard one seaman, and fractured the thigh of
> another. In about a minute she righted with the loss of fore-topsail-yard

Worse was to follow:

> At noon a tremendous sea struck the ship on the starboard beam, which threw
> her on her beam ends, with her tops in the water, dead lights a second time
> stove in, washed the Commander, Lt I. Binney, and myself with eleven
> seamen overboard. I being the only person out of the number who regained
> the ship...

Her commander and thirteen of the crew having been lost:

> ... the sea swept the ship from stem to stern-post, carrying everything away
> to the covering boards, which in many places were ripped up, obliging us to
> fill up between the timbers with oakum and wedges, to prevent her going
> down, having nothing above the gunwale but the starboard cat-head and
> anchor. In about two or three minutes the ship righted, with the loss of masts
> and bowsprit; found between five and six feet of water in her hold; employed
> pumping, securing the hatches, and clearing wreck from the ship, the sea
> making a complete breach over us...– James Brown

Had her masts not carried away, the **Star** would have
undoubtedly gone down with the loss of all hands, As it was she
remained in a perilous situation for three more days before her crew,
now under the direction of her sailing master, James Brown, got the
packet under command again. Unable to make Halifax, he was obliged
to make for Antigua, eventually reaching Nevis on December 24th.

By February 1836, further vessels of the new class were
reported as to be barque-rigged. The substitution of barques for brigs was
probably hastened by the **Star's** experience, and supports a previous
claim that these brigs were 'over-hatted'. That is to say they could carry
too much sail, and in addition the masts, spars and rigging were of
unnecessary strength. Excessive strength aloft could prove a fatal flaw
in the event of a vessel being blown down on to her beam ends. Lying
in such a perilous position, unless her sails blew out, or her masts and
rigging carried away, a vessel was unlikely to recover, and with deck
openings submerged would quickly fill and sink. As John Eastman, had
observed in May 1833:

> Having myself served as master nearly three years in his Majesty's packet-
> brig **Rinaldo**, I can truly say, without fear of contradiction by her present
> officers, that a safer or better sea-boat, or more sea-worthy vessel, is seldom
> to be met with ...

> ... few, if any, will carry away their masts, if properly rigged. The
> consequence is, that in hard squalls or increasing gales of wind, if due
> attention be wanting, the vessel is laid on her beam-ends, the yards will not
> come down, the men cannot stand to let go the ropes, the helm is rendered

useless. It may happen that the lee-ports are lashed in, and some of the hatches off: – in a few minutes the vessel sinks.

More new vessels followed, and the **Penguin**, launched at Pembroke naval dockyard on the 10th of April, 1838, was described as *... of a beautiful model, ...* by Sir William Symonds, the surveyor of the Navy: *her cabins are elegantly fitted with the mahogany saved from the old* **Gibraltar***...* Even in the naval packets, style and elegance were of some import. She and her consorts, the **Crane**, **Express**, **Linnet**, **Peterel** and **Swift**, formed the last generation of sailing packets based at Falmouth.

Back in 1823, shortly after the Admiralty had taken control of the packet service, a commercial company inaugurated a steam packet service between London and Seville, which marked the beginning of the end of the Falmouth to Lisbon packet route. While the paddle steamer **Royal George** was not an immediate commercial success, she paved the way for others to follow.

In 1836 steam competition commenced in earnest on this lucrative route, initially with a regular service between London and Malaga, calling at Falmouth, Gibraltar, Cadiz, Lisbon and Oporto, in either direction, with occasional diversions to Madeira. The following year the Peninsular Steam Navigation Company (PSNCo the forerunner of P&O), obtained a contract for a weekly service, carrying the Falmouth – Vigo, Oporto, Lisbon Cadiz and Gibraltar mails. This replaced the old monthly service, provided by Admiralty steam vessels to and from the Med., and the weekly sailing packets running between Falmouth and Lisbon. The Admiralty steam packets were now confined to the Mediterranean, where they provided a fortnightly link between Gibraltar, Malta, and Alexandria – carrying the India mails and other services.

The new service opened on September 4th 1837, to an inauspicious start, when their paddle steamer **Don Juan**, went ashore on Cape Tarifa, in thick fog on September 15th. She became a total wreck, though fortunately no lives were lost. The mail and £40,000 on freight were saved, and the PSNCo went on from strength to strength. For some years their steam packets continued to call at Falmouth, receiving and delivering their mails, which remained in the care and charge of a naval lieutenant for the duration of their respective voyages, and by March 1845 there were some 33 lieutenants acting as Admiralty agents on board contract steamers.

In June 1840 the postal authorities published a notice declaiming that:

The Packet Mails for North America will in future be despatched by Steam Vessels from Liverpool instead of Falmouth. The first Mail will be made up in London, on the 3rd July, ... The Packets will depart from Liverpool the next Morning as soon after the Arrival of the London Mail as possible ...

This notice marked the inauguration of the British & North American Royal Mail Steam Packet Company, otherwise known as the Cunard Line, and in January 1842, the Royal Mail Steam Packet Company vessels, sailing from Southampton, acquired the contract for the services to the West Indies, Mexico, and Cuba. Like the PSNCo, they were also obliged to call at Falmouth to pick up and land the mails – but not for long. Even though an effective steam railway service had been established between London and Southampton in May 1840, it took until September 1843 before approval was given for the mails to be sent to and from Southampton direct, when Falmouth was dropped as a port of call for these services.

A local steam feeder service having been established between Rio de Janeiro and Buenos Ayres, only six sailing brigs remained on the Falmouth station, maintaining the links with South America. These vessels did sterling work performing some remarkable voyages. In November 1842, HMB **Crane**, under Lt Lewis, RN, arrived at Falmouth in fourteen weeks and four days on a round voyage to Rio Janeiro. It was claimed as the shortest passage ever made and she brought home two cabin passengers (one a Russian Minister) and some miners, along with a freight of £19,000. Tramping home from Rio in 33 days, it was observed that: *When sailing Packets can make such voyages, the country will not require West India Steamers.* In fact this was not the fastest round voyage to Rio which honour remained with the late Lt Bullocke and the contract packet **Walsingham** (2), at 82 days back in August–November 1817. And, while this was the quickest passage since the Admiralty took control, such voyages could not prevent the wheels of progress from rolling right over the packet service.

Towards the end of 1850 the packet station at Falmouth was in the final stages of being wound up. The West India steamers had at last secured the South American contract, and the last but one of the sailing packets were all at sea on their final voyages. On the 6th December the HM Brig **Seagull**, under the command of Lt Smale, sailed for Brazil. She carried no passengers, but had a freight of £40,000.

The local paper of December 13th noted that, *The* **Swift**, *Lieut Lory, was to be paid off at Plymouth on Thursday, the 12th inst, ...and that* several of her crew had entered for the regular service. They went on:

> *We apprehend that the West Indian Company give the preference to applications from seamen paid off from Her Majesty's packet service, and will continue to do so for the new Brazilian line of steamers. Mr. Vincent commands the* **Severn** *steamship, and from his boyhood belonged to the packet establishment at this place, will proceed with the February Brazil mail, and the establishment of the route was committed to Mr. Valler, also of this port, and brought up in this now defunct establishment. Nevertheless there can be no doubt entertained, that should we be so fortunate as to have a direct*

Lt Thomas Baldock, RN
Another bluff packet
commander, Baldock
served towards the end
of the packet era
(1818–32).
Commanding both civil
and naval sailing
packets, he later went on
to command some of the
early steam vessels. He
is portrayed here in the
Naval uniform of the
1830s

railway communication with the metropolis, the whole packet communication would be again via Falmouth.

Hope sprang eternal, but there was no rescuing railway service in sight. Preparations were in hand to tow away the government coal hulk **Aurora**, and the late packet **Penguin**, had already been commissioned for service on the Coast of Africa. The **Express** was also to be placed on the same service:

> … *their compliment is to be 76 officers and men, and their armament 4–32lbs. carronades of 17 cwt., and 2 guns, 32 pounders of 32 cwt. on Hardy's slides. The* **Penguin** *will be in charge of a commander, on the important duty in which she is about to be employed – the suppression of the slave trade; and Commander Thomas Etheridge (1848), is appointed to her for that purpose.*

It is perhaps ironic that, the West India merchants' constant demand for the latest information from the slave plantations having led to the introduction of the West India packets in the first place, the last generation of these vessels were to be employed in the suppression of the slave trade.

The **Crane**, Lt Parsons, returned to Falmouth on Sunday December 29th, in 47 days from Rio, bringing home freight of about £10,000, and five passengers. On February 7th, 1851, the **Linnet**, Lt James, was reported to have arrived the previous Sunday, having taken

45 days running home from Rio, bringing a freight of £40,000, along with three passengers, and two miners!

The operation of weighing the depôt ship **Astrea's** anchors was carried out on Tuesday February 18th, and she was towed away to Plymouth that evening by HM steamer **Virago**. As the penultimate act, the **Peterel**, Lt Creser, came into Falmouth on the morning of Sunday March 9th, in 54 days from Rio. She had on board freight of just £6,000, with a Mr D Vega, and two miners, as passengers.

The final curtain call was reported in the *Royal Cornwall Gazette* of May 2nd, 1851:

> *On Wednesday morning the* **Seagull**, *Lieut Smale, arrived from Rio Janeiro, 47 days passage. She brought only a small parcel of letters, and but three packets of diamonds on freight; Passengers – Miss Lucy and Miss Mary Weitman, Master Le Febre, Mrs Fowler and three children, and Mr Manuel. The* **Tay** *steamer, having left Rio subsequently, her advices have been some days anticipated. This is the last vessel on this station as a packet, and with her this old and valuable station ceases to be the starting port of Her Majesty's mails, at least for the present.*

Despite this last lingering hope, after over 150 years in service the Falmouth Packet Station now closed. Steamships had finally driven the sailing packets from the seas. For a brief period during the 1914–18 war Falmouth once again acted as the terminal port for an emergency mail service to and from Bilboa. It was a brief respite, but no more. With this brief postal link with northern Spain the wheel of progress had almost turned a full circle.

The closure of the packet service after 150 years of operations from Falmouth meant inevitable hardship for the populace. Falmouth, abandoned as the hub of international communications, now had to re-establish itself, and the people had to re-build their own and the town's prosperity. The port and town of Falmouth have had their ups and downs since, and in some respects it has taken the port another 150 years to work off the packet legacy – and yet it is still a fascinating subject! However, the opening years of the 21st Century seem to be witnessing the beginning of a new cycle, and the commencement of a new era of prosperity for Falmouth.

Falmouth Packet War Time Compliments & Wages

		Costs in time of War. 1790				War Establishment now proposed : May 1791			
Rank/Rating	No	P-Ann Each	P-Lunar Month	P-Lunar Month	P-Ann Gross	No.	P-Ann Gross	P-Lunar Each	P Lunar Month	P Ann Gross
Commander	1	£104.00	£8.00	£8.00	£104.00	1	£104.00	£8.00	£8.00	£104.00
Master	1	£52.00	£4.00	£4.00	£52.00	1	£52.00	£4.00	£4.00	£52.00
Surgeon	1	£52.00	£4.00	£4.00	£52.00	1	£52.00	£4.00	£4.00	£52.00
1st Mate	1	£32.10s	£2.10s	£2.10s	£32.10s	1	£32.10s	£2.10s	£2.50	£32.10s
Carpenter	1	£32.10s	£2.10s	£2.10s	£32.10s	1	£32.10s	£2.10s	£2.50	£32.10s
2nd Mate	1	£26.00	£2.00	£2.00	£26.00					
Boatswain	1	£22.15s	£1.15s	£1.15s	£22.15s	1	£22.15s	£1.15s	£1.15s	£22.15s
Gunner	1	£22.15s	£1.15s	£1.15s	£22.15s	1	£22.15s	£1.15s	£1.15s	£22.15s
Boatswain's Mate	1	£19.10s	£1.10s	£1.10s	£19.10s					
Carpenter's Mate	1	£19.10s	£1.10s	£1.10s	£19.10s					
Cockswain	1	£19.10s	£1.10s	£1.10s	£19.10s					
Able Seamen	48	£18.4s	£1.8s	£67.4s	£873.12s	22	£18.4s	£1.8s	£30.16s	£400.8s
Ordinary	1	£13.00	£1.00	£1.00	£13.00					
Cook						1	£19.10s	£1.10s	£1.10s	£19s10s
Wage bill	**60**			**£99.4s**	**£1,289.12s**	**30**			**£56.16s**	**£738.8s**
		p-diem					p-diem			
Victualling	60	1s		£84.4s 7d	£1,095.00	30	1s		£42.2s 3d	£547.10s
Interest on first cost of £3,200 @ 5%										£160.00
Insurance @ 7%										£224.00
Hire, Wear, Tear and all Port charges				£94.13s 3d	£1,230.12s 6d				£36.18s 5d	£480.00
Gunpowder				£3.00	£39.00					
Use of Arms & Warlike stores				£12.4s	£158.12s					
Medicine Chest										£8.00
Additional 1s. allowance p-man/month for 60				£3.00	£39.00	30			£1.10s	£19.10s
Other Costs				£197.1s 9d	£2,562.4s 6d				£80.10s 9d	£1,439.00
Total Cost per Packet				**£296.5s 10d**	**£3,851.16s 6d**				**£137.6s 9d**	**£2,177.8s**
		Cost for 22 Packet Boats			£84,740. 3s		Cost for 18 Packet Boats			£39,193. 4s

For clarity parts of a penny have been ignored

Falmouth Packet Peace Time Compliments & Wages

Rank/Rating	No.	Costs in Peace time @ 1790 pay				Peace Establishment Proposed – 1791				
		P-Ann. Each	P-Lunar Month	P-Lunar Month Gross	P-Ann.	No Gross	P-Ann. Each	P-Lunar Month	P-Lunar Month Gross	P-Ann Gross
Commander	1	£78.00	£6.00	£6.00	£78.00	1	£78.00	£6.00	£6.00	£78.00
Master	1	£52.00	£4.00	£4.00	£52.00	1	£52.00	£4.00	£4.00	£52.00
Surgeon	1	£52.00	£4.00	£4.00	£52.00	1	£52.00	£4.00	£4.00	£52.00
Carpenter	1	£26.00	£2.00	£2.00	£26.00	1	£26.00	£2.00	£2.00	£26.00
1st Mate	1	£26.00	£2.00	£2.00	£26.00	1	£26.00	£2.00	£2.00	£26.00
Boatswain	1	£19.10s	£1.10s	£1.10s	£19.10s	1	£19.10s	£1.10s	£1.10s	£19.10s
Able Seamen Ordinary	24	£18.4s	£1.8s	£33.12s	£436.16s	15	£18.4s	£1.8s	£21.00	£273.00
Wage bill	**30**			**£53.2s**	**£690.6s**	**21**			**£40.10s**	**£526.10s**

		p-diem					p-diem			
Victualling	30	9d		£31.11s 8d	£410.12s 6d	21	9d		£22.2s 2d	£287.8s 9d
First cost of £4,000 @ 5% interest						On first cost of £3,200 @ 5% interest				
& decay @ 3%				£24.12s 6d	£320.00	& decay @ 3%			£12.6s 2d	£160.00
Insurance @ 7%				£21.10s 9d	£280.00				£17.4s 8d	£224.00
Hire, Wear, Tear				£40.00	£520.00				£32.00	£416.00
Medicine Chest				£0.9s 2d	£6.00				£0.6s 2d	£4.00
Additional 1s. allowance p-man/month for 30				£1.10s	£19.10s	21			£1.1s	£13.13s
Other Costs				£119.14s	£1,556.2s 6d				£85.0s 1d	£1,105.1s 10d
Cost per Packet				**£172.16s**	**£2,246.8s 6d**				**£125.10s.1d**	**£1,631.11s 9d**
		Cost for 22 Packet Boats			£49,421.7s	Cost for 18 Packet Boats				£29,368.11s 6d

For clarity parts of a penny have been ignored

Instructions for the guidance of the Captains and Crews of the Packets

By Command of the Right Honourable
THE POST-MASTER-GENERAL

RULES *to be observed by the Captains, Officers, and Seamen, belonging to his Majesty's Pacquet-Boats on the* FALMOUTH *Station.*

    First. *That when two, or more Pacquet-Boats meet in a foreign Port, the junior Captain shall wait on the senior immediately, and, if any Assistance to each other should be wanting, the senior Captain to have it in his power to order such number of hands from other Pacquet-Boats, as may be necessary to expedite the ship in turn of sailing*

    Secondly. *That every Captain of a Pacquet-Boat, coming into port from a voyage, shall give every seaman, belonging to his ship, who requests it, his discharge in writing, unless, the Captain of such Pacquet-Boat shall be ordered by the Agent to get ready for sea immediately; in which case, he shall be justified in refusing a discharge to the seamen.*

    Thirdly. *That no Captain of a Pacquet-Boat shall ship, or take on board his said Pacquet-Boat any seaman, not having such written discharge, except such man has not been before employed in the Pacque''s service.*

    Fourthly. *That in case of the desertion of any seaman from a Pacquet-Boat, the Captain shall be obliged before he sails on his next Voyage, to give in his name to the Agent's Clerk, to the end, that such Deserter may not again be employed in the Pacquet-Service, unless, directions shall be given to the contrary by a Committee; which Committee is to consist of the Agent with any three, or more Captains, then in the Port of Falmouth.*

    Fifthly. *That any Captain, having a complaints against a seaman for misbehaviour shall give in his name to that Agent, that a Committee may be called, who are to hear the complaint, with the seaman's defence, and give their opinion on the matter; And if it shall appear to them, that such seaman is no longer worthy of being employed in the Pacquet-Service, he shall not be received by any Captain on board his Pacquet-Boat; unless the Committee shall, on such seaman's making proper concession, think him worthy of being again taken into the service; in which case the Committee shall be impowered to grant him a certificate, on producing which, any Captain may again receive him on board his ship.*

    Sixthly. *That the Agent's Clerk for the time being, shall keep a regular list of the name, and description of every Seaman, who, any Captain may inform him, has deserted, or otherwise offended; And that such list shall always be produced by him at every muster on board the several Pacquet-Boats.*

    Seventhly. *That a Captain, having anything to propose for the benefit of the service, shall apply to the Agent, who shall, as soon as conveniently may be, call a Committee of Captains, then in port, of which he is at all times to be the president, when such Captain shall give in his proposals in writing to the Committee.*

    Eighthly. *That every Captain, being duly Summoned by the Agent's order, shall attend the Committee; unless he gives a satisfactory excuse to the members thereof.*

    Ninethly. *That every seaman, whilst employed in the Pacquet-Service, thinking himself ill used or aggrieved by any Captain of a Pacquet-Boat, may apply to the Agent for the time being, who shall immediately summon a Committee, and hear each party, and make report thereon, and grant such relief, as they shall see proper.*

    Tenthly. *That these articles be lodged, and deposited for the benefit of all parties with the Agent of the Pacquet-Boats, for the time being, whose Clerk shall read the same, or true copies thereof, publicly, at every muster. And, that **these** Articles shall commence, and take place from the twenty-second day of October next.*

By Command, STEPHEN BELL, Agent.

Dated July 22nd 1782

Falmouth Packets Victualling 1790

A Statement of the Quantity & Value of Provisions allowed to each Seaman for each day in the Week in H
Majesty' s Service – c.1790.

	Bread		Beer		Beef		Pork		Pease		Oatmeal		Value of day
	lb	Value	Quart	Value	lb	Value	lb.	Value	Gall.	Value	Pints	Val	
Sun	1	1½d	4	4¾d			1	4¼d	½	¾d			11¼d
Mon	1	1½d	4	4¾d							1	1½d	7¾d
Tues	1	1½d	4	4¾d	2	6d							1s 0¼d
Wed	1	1½d	4	4¾d					½	¾d	1	1½d	8½d
Thurs	1	1½d	4	4¾d			1	4¼d	½	¾d			11¼d
Fri	1	1½d	4	4¾d					½	¾d	1	1½d	8½d
Sat	1	1½d	4	4¾d	2	6d							1s 0¼d
Total Per man per week													
	7	10½d	28	2s 9¼d	4	1s	2	8½d	2	3d	3	4½d	5s 11¾d

Statement of the Cost of Purchasing Victuals at Falmouth in 1812 – submitted to the Post Office Board by the Packet Commanders

A Statement of the prices of provisions at Falmouth in June 1812 and for many months preceding

Beef per-Barrell of 190 lbs.		£6 5s
Pork per-Barrell of190 lbs.		£5 15s
Average of at per-Barrell - -	£6 which is	7½d per lb
Butter		1s 2d per lb
Bread	54/- p-Cwt	6d per lb
Pease	p-Gallon	2s per qt
Flour	p-Pound	5d per lb

Expences of One Weeks Victualling each Seaman on the Falmouth Station

7lbs Beef or Pork	4s 4½d	
1/2 lb Butter	7d	
7lbs Bread	3s 6d	
1 quart Pease	6d	
2lbs Flour	10½d	
Total	**9s 10d**	**which is 17d per day per-Man**
Allowance by the		
Establishment at 10d	5s 1d	

Loss sustained weekly by a Captain for each Man Ammounting to £298-1-8 p-Annum besides Coals and Candles

Report of a Committee of Captains 1813

At a Committee of Captains held at
the Packet Office the 31st May 1813.
Present

   Christopher Saverland Esq.r – Chairman
  Captains Lawrance
      Bell
      Elphinstone
      Naylor
      Stevens
      White
      Parsons
      Kirkness
      Davey
      Quick
      Harvey

This Committee was called by order of the Post Master General to enquire into the circumstances of the Capture of the **Mary Ann** Packet Captain James Caddy as also the loss of the Mails on her Voyage from Gibraltar when we proceeded to examine the Mate, Boatswain, Gunner, Carpenter and Steward of that Packet and it appeared that she was taken by the **General Tompkin** American Privateer pierced for Sixteen and mounting ten long Nine Pounders and one long twenty-four pounder amidships with a crew composed of Ninety nine men – and that he defended the Packet in a most gallant manner to the utmost of his power until she was perfectly unmanageable and we do therefore most honorably acquit Capt.n Caddy his Officers and Crew of any blame attaching to them on account of the Capture of the said Packet –

And that in respect of the loss of the Mail it appears to this Committee that it must have happened from the Mails containing a number of Boxes which made it more buoyant that it would otherwise have been, as the usual weight was attached to the Mails of the **Mary Ann**, which has hitherto been always understood in this service to be sufficient for the purpose of sinking it – And this Committee are confirmed in their opinion that such was the Case, as the **Hinchinbrook** Packet from Gibraltar which immediately followed the **Mary Ann**
had a number of Boxes in her Mail. –

   C. Saverland
   Edw.d Lawrance   Step. Bell
   Rob.t Naylor   R. P. R. Elphinstone
   Ja.s Stevens   Jo.s White
   Simon Davey,   Wm. Kirkness
   John Parsons   Rich.d Harvey
   John Quick.

A true Copy of the original – J N Tippet – Secretary to the Captain's Committee.

Rates for Passengers on the Falmouth Packets 1810

STATIONS	VOYAGES	CABIN	STEERAGE
LISBON	To or from Falmouth & Lisbon	£22.1s 0	£13 13s 0
CADIZ	To or from Falmouth and Cadiz	£32 11s 0	£18 18s 0
MEDITERRANEAN	From Falmouth to Gibraltar	£37 16s 0	£21 10s 6
	From Falmouth to Cagliari	£56 14s 0	£30 19s 6
	From Falmouth to Girgenti or Malta	£58 16s 0	£32.0s 6
	From Falmouth to Messina	£60 18s 0	£33 1s 6
	To or from Gibraltar and either of the above Places		
		£27 6s 0	£14 19s 3
	From Sicily, Malta or Cagliari to Falmouth	£64 1s 0	£34 13s 0
	From Gibraltar to Falmouth	£48 6s 0	£26 15s 6
BRAZILS	From Falmouth to Madeira	£37 16s 0	£21 10s 6
	From Falmouth to Brazils	£85 1s 0	£45 3s 0
	From Madeira to Brazils	£53 11s 0	£29 8s 0
	From Brazils to Falmouth	£106 1s 0	£55 13s 0
AMERICA	To or from Falmouth and Halifax	£53 11s 0	£29 8s 0
	To or from New York direct	£53 11s 0	£29 8s 0
	To New York by Halifax	£58 16s 0	£32 0s 0
	From New York, by Halifax to Falmouth	£58 16s 0	£32 0s 0
	From Falmouth to Bermuda	£53 11s 0	£29 8s 0
JAMAICA	From Falmouth to Barbadoes or Martinique	£53 11s 0	£29 8s 0
	From Falmouth to Curacoa	£58 16s 0	£32 0s 0
	From Falmouth to Jamaica	£58 16s 0	£32 0s 0
	Fron Jamaica to Falmouth	£53 11s 0	£29 8s 0
LEEWARD ISLANDS	From Falmouth to Barbadoes or Martinique	£53 11s 0	£29 8s 0
	From Falmouth to Dominica	£54 12s 0	£19 18s 0
	From Falmouth to Guadeloupe	£55 13s 0	£30 9s 0
	From Falmouth to Antigua	£57 15s 0	£31 10s 0
	From Falmouth to Montserrat	£58 16s 0	£32 0s 6
	From Falmouth to Nevis or St. Kitts	£60 18s 0	£33 1s 6
	From Falmouth to Tortola or St. Thomas's	£63 0s 0	£34 2s 6
	From any of the above Islands to Falmouth	£53 11s 0	£29 8s 0
SURINAM, &c	From Falmouth to Surinam	£56 14s 0	£30 19s 6
	From Falmouth to Berbice	£57 15s 0	£31 10s 0
	From Falmouth to Demerara	£58 16s 0	£32 0s 6
	From either of the above places to Falmouth	£53 11s 0	£29 8s 0

Female servants pay as Cabin Passengers: Children under 12 Months of Age go free of Charge; under 4 Years of Age pay as Steerage; above 4 Years as Cabin Passengers. The Passengers by all except the Lisbon Packets, provide Bedding; and from the West Indies lay in their own Stock. Each Passenger allowed to carry any Weight of Linen; Wearing Apparel and Books, not exceeding 400 Lbs. Any Commander of a Packet, demanding more than the above authorized Rates, will incur the high displeasure of my Lords the Postmaster General
November, 1810.   C. SAVERLAND, Agent.

Rates for Passengers on the Falmouth Packets 1835

STEAM VESSELS		CABIN	STEERAGE
PORTUGAL	To or from Falmouth & Lisbon or Oporto	£12 0s	£6 10s
MEDITERRANEAN	From Falmouth to Cadiz or Gibraltar	£17 0s	£9 10s
	From Falmouth to Malta	£29 0s	£16 0s
	From Falmouth to Corfu	£36 0s	£20 0s
	To or from Gibraltar and Malta	£14 0s	£8 0s
	To or from Gibraltar and Corfu	£22 0s	£12 0s
	To or from Malta and Patras	£8 0s	£5 0s
	To or from Malta and Corfu via Patras	£10 0s	£6 0s
	To or from Malta and Corfu direct	£8 0s	£5 0s
	To or from Malta and Alexandria	£10 0s	£6 0s
	From Corfu to Falmouth	£36 0s	£20 0s
	From Malta to Falmouth	£29 0s	£19 0s
	From Gibraltar or Cadiz to Falmouth	£17 0s	£9 10s

SAILING PACKETS			
BRAZILS AND BUENOS AYRES			
	From Falmouth toMadeira	£25 0s	£13 0s
	Do. Teneriffe	£27 0s	£14 0s
	To or from Falmouth & Pernambuco	£49 0s	£25 0s
	Do. and Bahia	£52 0s	£27 0s
	Do. & Rio Janeiro via Pernambuco and Bahia	£57 0s	£30 0s
	Do.and Buenos Ayres (via Do.)	£75 0	£38 0s
	Do. and Rio Janeiro, direct	£52 0s	£24 0s
	Do. & Buenos Ayres & Rio Janeiro, direct	£70 0s	£36 0s
	To or fromBuenos Ayres & Rio Janeiro	£20 0s	£12 0s
NORTH AMERICA			
	From Falmouth to Halifax	£30 0s	£16 0s
	From Falmouth to Bermuda, (via Halifax)	£40 0s	£21 0s
	To or from Halifax and Bermuda	£12 0s	£7 0s
	From Bermuda to Falmouth, (via Halifax)	£35 0s	£18 0s
	From Halifax to Falmouth, (via Halifax)	£28 0s	£15 0s
WEST INDIES, CARTHAGENA, AND MEXICO			
	From Falmouth to Barbadoes	£35 0s	£18 0s
	From Falmouth to Dominica or Guadeloupe	£37 0s	£19 0s
	From Falmouth to Antigua or Montserrat	£38 0s	£20 0s
	From Falmouth to Nevis or St. Kitts	£39 0s	£21 0s
	From Falmouth to Tortola, St. Thomas, or Jamaica	£40 0s	£22 0s
	From Falmouth to Havannah	£43 0s	£22 0s
	From Falmouth to Carthagena or Honduras	£46 0s	£23 0s
	From Falmouth to Vera Cruz or Tampico	£52 0s	£27 0s
	From St. Thomas to Falmouth, (via Halifax)	£40 0s	£20 0s
	From Jamaica or Houduras to Falmouth	£52 0s	£27 0s
	From Carthagena to Falmouth, (via Halifax)	£58 0s	£29 0s
	From Vera Cruz to Falmouth, (via Halifax)	£60 0s	£30 0s

STEAM VESSELS

		CABIN	STEERAGE
From Barbadoes to Jamaica		£10 0s	£6 0s
From Jamaica to St. Thomas		£10 0s	£6 0s
From St. Thomas to Barbadoes (direct)		£5 0s	£3 0s

Intermediate passages not mentioned, to be paid proportionable with the above, in reference to time and distance. Female servants to pay one-third of the cabin-passage money. Men servants as steerage passengers. Children under three year of age to go free; under nine years of age, to pay as steerage passengers; and above nine years, as cabin passengers when belonging to such. Each passenger allowed to carry any weight of linen, wearing apparel, and books, not exceeding 400 lbs. Passengers not proceeding after taking their passage forfeit half their passage-money. Bedding in sailing packets to be found by the passengers. The passage-money to be so paid as to realize the sterling money in England.

No carriages to be carried in sailing packets. All former rates to be cancelled. The Lieutenants commanding steam-vessels are to pay to the public one-third of the passage money, as heretofore, up to the number of twelve cabin passengers, and for all exceeding that number one-half to be paid to the public

An Account of the Freight per Sundry Packets received at the Bullion Office on Account of the Post Office being 1/3 part of said Freight

1811	Names	Port	Total Amount of Freight	Post Office Proportion
03 Sep	**Lord Chesterfield** (3)	St. Thomas	£558 18s 6d	£186 6s 2d
03 Sep	**Princess Elizabeth** (3)	Martinique	£27 12s 7d	£9 4s 2d
03 Sep	**Adventure**	Jamaica	£185 3s 0d	£61 14s 4d
12 Sep	**Prince of Wales**	Jamaica	£637 6s 0d	£106 4s 4d
14 Sep	**Earl of Sandwich**(2)	Rio	£34 5s 0d	£11 8s 4d
15 Sep	**Express**	Gibraltar	£23 0s 0d	£7 13s 4d
22 Sep	**Diana**	Martinique	£42 3s 0d	£14 0s 1d
29 Sep	**Queen Charlotte** (3)	St. Thomas some freight paid at Falmouth		
			£184 15s 0d	£61 11s 8d
30 Sep	**Speedy** (2)	Rio some freight paid abroad		
			£369 15s 7d	£123 5s 2d
03 Oct	**Princess Mary**	Jamaica	£797 11s 3d	£265 17s 1d
13 Oct	**Eliza**	Martinique	£58 17s 0d	£19 12s 4d
18 Oct	**Lady Arrabella**	Rio some freight paid abroad		
			£331 13s 0d	£110 11s 0d
02 Nov	**Darlington**	St. Thomas some freight paid at Plymouth		
			£98 18s 0d	£32 19s 4d
18 Nov	**Prince Adolphus**	Jamaica	£793 16s 0d	£264 12s 0d
02 Dec	**Manchester**	Martinique	£32 0s 10d	£10 13s 7d
13 Dec	**Duke of Montrose** (2)	Rio some freight paid at Rio		
			£651 18s 7d	£217 6s 2d
23 Dec	**Mary Ann**	St. Thomas	£158 3s 8d	£52 14s 6d
TOTAL			**£4985 14s 1d**	**£1555 13s 7d**

Packet Seamen's Petition 1806

To the Right Honorable the Lords of the Treasury –

The humble Petition of the Seamen belonging to the **Duke of Montrose, Princess Charlotte, Hobart,** and **Princess Augusta,** Packets on the Falmouth Station –

Sheweth

That by order of the Commifsioners of his Majesty's Customs your Petitioners are Prohibited from taking out little Adventures of Cheese, Potatoes, Shoes, &c. of British Manufacture in the Packets to the British Colonies, by which means your Petitioners hitherto derived some small Advantage, for the maintenance of their families – but being now deprived of it they have most humbly to state to your Lordships that they have been bred in the Packets service and have ably and cheerfully defended their Ships on various occasions, that a great many of your Petitioners have large families and only thirty shillings and six pence per month Wages and six pence per day Victualling Money Whilst in the Harbour of Falmouth but in no other Harbour, on which it is impofsible for their families to subsist, without being permitted to take out the above trifles as a private Adventure – That large quantities of British Manufactured Goods are permitted to be exported by the Lisbon Packets both of Freight and as private Adventures, by which means the Seamen on that station are enabled to maintain their Families in comfort whilst your Petitioners Wives and Children are experiencing penury and distrefs –

Your Petitioners therefore throw themselves on your Lordships humanity and compafsion most humbly requesting you will take their hard case into consideration and direct that these little Advantages which they have hitherto enjoyed they may not now be deprived

And your Petitioners will every pray &c. –

Falmouth 25th August 1806.

Thos. Tregaronan	Peter Tucker	N. Tresise
Geo. Trerilson	William Williams	Daniel Roe
James Creale	James Mitchel	Thomas Thomas
P Dupen	John Coplin	John Cuttance
Joseph Saxton	Richard Wilson	Alexander Thomas
W Sutton	Stephen Puling	John Ralph
Wm Pearce	Henery Hutton	Philip Andrew
John Bailey	Thomas Alen	Richard Caddy
John Fofset	John Carter	John Moor
James Millett	Abraham Dixon	Hangen Holm
Samuel Pulvin	William Pollard	William Gidley
George George	James Robinson	John Rowling
John Gill	Charles Harry	Henry Gundry/Gandry
John Kitto	Charles Newman	James Nankivel
John Morgan	Henry Williams	Frank Mitchell
George Bickland	John Cornish	Soloman Martin
Samuel Martn	James Mitchell	

List of Falmouth Packet Losses under Admiralty Control

Cynthia a purchased packet, with 32 persons on board. Under the command of Lt White, RN she left Falmouth for Jamaica on May 7th 1827, only to become wrecked on the island of Barbados or June 6th 1827. The accident occurred in moderate weather, and all on board were saved.

Hearty a 10-gun brig, with 35 persons on board. Sailed from Falmouth for Jamaica, under the command of Lt Jawry/Jewry, RN, on September 12th 1827. Was spoken by a passing vessel in the N E Trades, within a few days sail of Barbados, but never reached that island. Was declared to have been burned, *the sailing master being in the habit of smoking in bed.*

Redpole a 10-gun brig, number of persons on board not known. Left Rio de Janeiro for Falmouth, under the command of Lt Bullocke, RN, on August 10th 1828. Due at Falmouth about the end of September, she never arrived. Her name was continued in the Packet List for many months, and the *Royal Cornwall Gazette* made a number of passing reports:

22/11/1828 – *We have still to regret that no intelligence respecting the safety of the* Redpole *Packet, Capt Bullocke, has reached England.*

29/11/1928 – *We are sorry to observe that another week has elapsed without any tidings of the* Redpole *packet, for the safety of which very slender hopes can now be entertained.*

Eventually all hope was abandoned, and she was presumed to have foundered with all hands. However, much later a survivor made a deposition to the effect that – she had been attacked off Cape Frio by the **Congress**, an 18-gun pirate vessel (or insurgent privateer) out of Buenos Ayres. After an engagement of one and a quarter hours she was sunk. No information was given as to any other survivors

Ariel a 10-gun brig, with 34 persons on board. Left Falmouth for Halifax, under the command of Lt John Figg, RN, on November 10th 1828. Some weeks later, in December, she was seen from a trading schooner out of Halifax, sailing directly towards Sable Island. Mr. Dulen, master of the schooner, tried to warn her off, but was unable to get close to her. She is supposed to have run on shore on Sable Island a few hours later. All on board were lost.

Myrtle a 10-gun brig, with 29 persons on board. Was returning to Falmouth from St. Domingo, under the command of Lt Sisson, RN, when she was wrecked on the coast of Nova Scotia on April 3rd 1829. The accident occurred in moderate weather, and all on board were saved.

Calypso a 10-gun brig, number of persons on board not known. Left Halifax for Falmouth, under the command of Lt Peyton, RN, on January 29th 1833, and was last seen surrounded by ice, from a fishing boat, the day after she sailed. She was evidently in distress, as she was firing her guns, but the fishing boat could not get near her because of the ice. Lost with all hands.

Recruit a 10-gun brig, number of persons on board not known. Left Halifax for England (or Bermuda – accounts vary), under the command of Lt Hodges, RN, on May 29th 1832, and was never seen or heard of again. Lost with all hands

Thais a 10-gun brig, with 35 persons on board. Left Falmouth for Halifax, under the command of Lt Charles Church, RN, on December 12th 1833. Meeting a succession of westerly gales; by a letter to Capt King (which presumably was discovered in the wreckage) by December 24th she was in 50° N. lon. 16° 8' W. lat. heading northward with the wind in the WNW. Some time later her launch and other wreckage came ashore on the West north coast of Ireland.

Briseis a 10-gun brig, with an undisclosed number of persons on board. She left Falmouth for Halifax on January 4th 1838, under the command of Lt J. Downey, RN, never to arrive. Again it was some time before all hope was abandoned, but the *Royal Cornwall Gazette*, of Friday, May 4th 1838 reported:

It is again our melancholy duty to state that there is no account of the **Briseis**. She had not been heard of at Halifax, up to the 2nd of April, when the **Hercules**, 74, which has arrived at Plymouth, left that port: nor, indeed, does a subsequent arrival at Portsmouth bring any news of her. The authorities in Nova Scotia had sent a vessel round Sable Island, to discover, if possible, whether she had been wrecked there. – Surely, there will at length be a stop put to the employment of ten-gun brigs in the Packet Service. A most painful experience has shewn their utter unfitness *for it: and nothing but a criminal carelessness of human life can prevent their being all laid aside before the approach of another winter.*

And the following week:

… **Briseis** …*there seems scarcely any ground to doubt that she has perished. Nearly all the crew were Falmouth-men; most of them married – the Commander to (Susan) a daughter of the late R. Symonds, esq., of Little Falmouth – and among the number, several were brothers, and some were sons of aged widows. No similar calamity has caused in this town, an affliction so extensive and so severe.*

Lord Melville the last civil packet in the service. Sailed from Falmouth for Halifax on October 5th 1839, under the command of Lt Charles Webbe, RN (married to Mary nee Symonds, sister to Susan Downey – above). The **Lord Melville** was never seen or hear of again, being lost with all hands.

When examined en-bloc it can be seen that there were various causes of loss, some apparent and others implied – though just why it was decided that the **Cynthia** was lost by fire, and that this was caused by her master 'smoking in bed', defies reason. In many instances there was no clear cut reason for their disappearance, and many months of speculation followed each loss. Just like the 'Bermuda Triangle' in modern times, there were many theories put forward, with some quite vociferous camps siding with one idea or another. The most likely common cause put forward was that they were all *Admiralty 10-gun brigs*, vessels quite unsuited to their duties. However, this was not the case, as at least two of them were civil vessels, albeit under the command of Royal Navy Lieutenants. Probably the most common element was human error – or more correctly human nature.

Under direct Admiralty command, there was much to be proved. Their ships were not ideal for the job in hand, but these RN packet commanders were under considerable pressure to deliver, to make fast passages and to maintain tight voyaging schedules. There were reputations to be won, and careers to be made, and perhaps too many were tempted to crack on in extreme conditions!

Bibliography

Atton & Holland, *The King's Customs* (2 Vols), Frank Cass & Co., London 1967
Beck, John, *Captain John Bull*, South West Maritime History Society, Exeter 1995
Beck, John, 'International Mail: The Falmouth Packet Service' Cornwall Maritime Museum Falmouth 1995
Britnor, Leonard E, *The Sailing Packets of the West Indies*, British West India Study Centre, London 1973
Cometti, Elizabeth (Ed), *The American Journals of Lt. John Enys*, Syracuse University Press, Syracuse 1976
Fellowes, William Dorset, A *Narrative of the Loss of His Majesty's Packet, the Lady Hobart, on an Island of Ise in the Atlantic Ocean*, John Stockdale, London 1803
Gay, Susan E, *Old Falmouth*, Headley Brothers, London 1903
Henderson, James, *Sloops & Brigs*, Leo Cooper, London 1972
Howat, Rev. JNT, *South American Packets 1808–1880*, William Sessions, York 1984
Kelly, Samuel (Ed Crosbie Garstin), *An Eighteenth Century Seaman*, Jonathan Cape Ltd., London 1925
Mudd, David, *The Falmouth Packets*, Bossiney Books, Bodmin 1978
Norway, Arthur, *History of the Post Office Packet Service*, Macmillan & Co., London 1895
Palmer, June, *Cornwall, the Canaries & the Atlantic*, Institute of Cornish Studies, Exeter 1997
Philbrick, ME, 'The Packet Captains of Flushing' Truro 1982
Robinson, Howard, *Carrying British Mail Overseas*, George Allen & Unwin Ltd., Liverpool 1964
Redwood, UM, 'Trefusis Territory' Falmouth 1987
Staff, Frank, *The Transatlantic Mail*, Allard Coles Ltd., London 1956
Tabeart, Colin, *Admiralty Mediterranean Steam Packets 1830 to 1857*, James Bendon Ltd., Limasol 2002
Uring, Nathaniel, *The Voyages and Travells of Captain Nathaniel Uring*, Cassell & Co. Ltd., London 1928
Whetter, JCA, *The History of Falmouth*, Dyllansow Truran 1987

Articles in Journals

Bowring, KWM, 'Flushing, 1840–1860', *History Around the Fal*, Falmouth 1980
Brindley, HH, 'The Loss of the *Lapwing* Post Office Packet' *Mariner's Mirror*, Vol.16, No.1 London 1930
Fisher, Stephen, 'Lisbon as a Port Town' *Exeter Maritime Studies* 2 Exeter 1988
Jago, Rev W, 'The Heroes of the Old Falmouth Packet Service' Journal of the *Royal Institution of Cornwall*, Vol.XIII, pt.II Truro 1896
Kemble, John Haskell, 'England's First Atlantic Mail' *Mariner's Mirror* Vol XXVI London 1940
Pawlyn, Tony, 'In Breach of Quarantine, the Falmouth Packet *Montagu*', *Maritime South West*, No 16
Philbrick ME, 'The Post Office Packet Service from Falmouth' *History Around the Fal* Falmouth 1980
Philbrick ME, 'Some Falmouth Packet Captains 1729–1832' *History Around the Fal* 2 Falmouth 1982
Philbrick ME, 'Falmouth Packet Captains (Couse, Sharp, Roberts, & Porteous)' *History Around the Fal* 3 Falmouth 1984
Philbrick ME, 'The Falmouth Post Office Packets' *History Around the Fal* 4 Falmouth 1986
Philbrick, ME, 'The Falmouth Packet Service' *Postal History Bulletin* No.207 1978
Whetter, JCA, 'Daniel Gwin – The First Agent of the Falmouth Packet Station' *Old Cornwall Journal* Autumn 1964
Yescombe, Edward, 'English and Particularly English Seamen', *Maritime South West*, No 16

Primary Sources

Cornwall Gazette Falmouth 1801 1802
Exeter Flying Post Exeter
Gentleman's Magazine London 1731
Lloyd's Lists London 1740
London Gazette London
Nautical Magazine 1832
Royal Cornwall Gazette Truro 1803
Sherborne Mercury Sherborne 1740
The Alfred Plymouth
United Services Magazine 1830
West Briton Truro 1810
Woolmer's Exeter Gazette Exeter

Papers

Relating to the Action between the PELHAM and MONTAGU Packets, and the GLOBE American Privateer. (2 November 1813.) British Parliamentary Papers (BPP) London 1815
Minutes of Evidence On Steam Navigation to India BPP London 1834
Post Office Packets BPP – LVIII; pp.507–528 London 1835
Post Office Steam Packets BPP – London 1839
Holyhead & Kingstown Mail Packets BPP. London 1852
Contracts: Royal Mail Steamers BPP London 1852
Falmouth Packet Establishment BPP – XXVII; pp.595–608 London 1831–2

Glossary

Abaft   Located behind, or towards the stern of, any point on a ship. i.e.– 'Abaft the main mast'. 'Abaft the beam'

Abeam   Across the width of the vessel; or a shipboard object lying beside another; or an imaginary point projected beyond the confines of the vessel

Aloft   Up in the rigging, or above decks

Alow   Below decks, within the hull of the vessel

Articles   Articles of Agreement. The formal contract terms under which merchant seamen served, and which they signed or made their 'mark' at the commencement of a voyage to acknowledge their agreement

Beam ends   A vessel laid on her side, usually by effect of wind and weather, and often with her cargo shifted, so that her deck (and deck-beams) were nearly vertical. Nearly capsized

Bittacle   Westcountry term for a binnacle, the housing for the steeering compass

Bloody flag   The blood red flag flown to indicate that no quarter would be offered to any enemy who otherwise survived the fight. An inducement to surrender before a fight commenced

Boarding netting   Curtains of loose netting suspended from the yard arms, making it dificult for attackers to board a vessel

Boarding pikes   Seven foot long timber staves headed by a seven inch iron spike. A long reach thrusting weapon, used to beat off would be enemy boarders

Boatswain's Call   The whistle used to convey orders to the crew. Distinctive trills, and alterations in pitch and intensity having well understood meanings on board ships

Breachings   Short lengths of strong rope, fastened to the hull of the ship and gun carriages, limiting their backwards travel under recoil

Brill   The English name for the Netherlands port of Brielle

Bulwarks or gunwale   The planking forming the side of a ship, above the upper deck

Burthen (tonnage) or Burden   The notional carrying capacity of the vessel. The estimated number of wine tuns that could be stowed in the hold

Butcher's bill   A euphemism for the list of killed and wounded (on either side), published after an action at sea. By which the general public determined the relative skill, bravery and merit of the combatants

Cannister   Cans of broken pieces of cast iron, designed to scatter when fired from a cannon, causing the maximum casualties to an enemy crew, and also to lacerate sails and rigging

Cannon / Carronades   Main armament guns. Sea service cannon & carronades, were classed by the weight of 'round shot' they fired. In the case of the Falmouth packets, anything from 3-pounder cannon, to 12-pounder carronades

Carriage guns   Main weaponry guns, set on heavy timber carriages mounted on solid wood wheels, or trucks. Usually worked with a limited field of fire through gun ports

Carronades   Short, broad bore, cannon, reputedly designed by the Carron Iron Company. Lacking accuracy over any distance, these small guns packed a heavy punch, and could be reloaded quicker than normal cannon. Despite their detractors, they were particularly handy on the decks of such small vesels as the packets

Cathead   A short, square sectioned spar, projecting over either bow of a vessel, by which an anchor is suspended ready for use. In early times the end of this spar was carved with the head of a cat

Chasers, Bow Chasers, or Stern Chasers   Long, relatively light carriage guns, set in the bow or stern as either attacking or defensive weapons respectively. Their shot carried further and straighter than shorter guns, and the objective was usually to shoot away spars, rigging or sails, to slow down the enemy. Often cast in bronze, these had the smoothest internal barrels, and thus the greatest accuracy

Chatham Chest   A national fund set up for the maintenance of sick and injured seamen, but usually restricted to ex Royal Navy personnel

Clew or Clue   Lowest point of attachment on a sail, to which is attached a 'sheet' for trimming the sail, or a 'clew line' to help furl the sail

Coamings   The raised edge around deck openings which prevents small amounts of free surface water from cascading below as a ship pitches and rolls

Cockpit   One of the more sheltered and secure places in a ship, located below the waterline

Copper sheathing   Sheets of copper tacked to the underwater hull of a ship, to prevent marine boring molluscs from eating away the planks and frames. Usually only fitted to vessels working in tropical or equatorial waters

Covering boards   The wide strip of planking running round a vessel, where the deck abuts against the hull planking, through which rise the stanchions which carry the bulwarks

Deadlights   A stout timber covers, that could be secured over skylights in rough weather

Decklights   Thick prisms of glass (perhaps twelve by four inches) that could be set into a deck to allow a small amout of light to permeate below

Droits of the Crown, or Admiralty   When enemy ships and cargoes were captured, they had to be condemned as Lawful Prize, in the High Courts of Admiralty, before the could be sold for the benefit of the captors. If captured by an unlicenced privateer or civil ship (technically a pirate), the seized property devolved to the Crown as their 'Right' or 'Droit'. This right was usually devolved to the Admiralty

Foot   The bottom edge of a sail

Freeboard   The nominal height of the main deck above the water line

Grape shot   Bags of musket balls or similar lead shot, designed to scatter when fired from a cannon, cutting a swathe of casualties through an enemy crew

Gunwale or bulwarks   The planking forming the side of a ship, above the upper deck

Hammock netting(s)   On packets : troughs of netting, secured inside the rails of a vessel, in which the crews' hammocks were stowed during action stations, giving some protection from flying splinters

Hatches   Openings in the deck, usually surrounded by a raised coaming, that could be covered by stout hatch-boards, and rendered waterproof with canvas covers battened down

Head   The top edge of a sail – usually a square or quadrilateral one

Holystoning   Scrubbing down the decks with 'bible', or 'prayer-book', sized blocks of abrasive sandstone. Working on hands and knees in running salt water

Iron pigs   Cast iron blocks, pig-iron, carried as sinkers for weighing down the mail portmanteaus

Larboard   An early term for the left hand side of a vessel when facing forwards. Officially replaced by 'port' in 1844, to avoid phonetic confusion with 'starboard'

Lee shore   The shore onto which the wind is blowing, hence rough and dangerous for shipping

Lee side   The side of the vessel away from the wind, where the hull was deepest emersed

Leech   The edge of a sail trailing away from the wind

Leeward   In a direction away from the wind

Letters of Marque, or Privateering Commission   Licences granted by states or countries to commanders of civil ships, to carry arms and to attack and capture enemy ships and cargoes as prizes of war. Originally 'tit for tat' reprisals, but by this period they were granted to general commerce raiders. Often considered legalised piracy

Light money   A levy imposed on shipping to pay the running costs of the lighthouse service

Log (perpetual)   A mechanical device, intended to give a continual reading of distance travelled by a vessel through the water, and by calculation the vessel's speed

Log Book   A vessel's official record, noting weather conditions; distance and direction sailed; observations of the sun, moon and stars; bearings and distance from land; & calculations of noon positions. Together with remarks on sails set, and any other remarkable occurances

Log line   A free running length of line, marked at measured intervals, by which the speed of a vessel through the water could be calculated

Luff   The edge of a square sail hauled up towards the wind; or the forward edge of a sail secured to a stay or mast

Offing   The sea area off a port or harbour, which vessels tried to clear as quickly as possible to avoid the danger of shipwreck

On freight (bullion)   The commercial carriage of bullion on freight terms – that is under payment for value or weight.

Pikemen   Hands armed with 'boarding pikes' whose task at action stations was to prevent enemy hands from getting on board their vessel

Poop   A small raised deck, over the quarter deck, at the stern of larger vessels. Sometimes used loosely to mean the back end of the quarterdeck on smaller flush-decked vessels

Port   The left hand side of a vessel, when standing with your back to the stern and facing the bow

Privateer, or Private Ship of War   Civil vessels, specially built or adapted for fighting, which had been granted 'letters of marque' to cruise against the shipping of a specified enemy

Quarterdeck   That part of the upper deck abaft the mainmast and restricted to the use of the officers, except when specific duties required the presence of seamen. A term usually restricted to warships

Sale by the candle   A form of auction, which commences when a short candle stub is lit, and closes with the last bid made before the flame goes out

Sheet   A single line, or purchase, attached to the lowest point of the leech of a sail (trailing edge), for trimming it to the wind

Ship mail   Letters carried by general merchant ships. Usually on routes not served by official mail packets

Shrouds   The standing rigging set on either side of a mast to give lateral support

Skylights   A small hatchway in the deck with raised coamings, closed by a hinged glazed top (or a pair of), and protected by a deadlight(s)

Slush   A foul concoction of fatty scum recovered from boiled meat and pork used as a lubricant. So much rancid fat was recovered, that the cooks stored the excess, and sold it at the end of each voyage as a perk = **Slush money**

Slushing down   Greasing those parts of a mast, where the yards were hoisted or lowered, with slush

Smashers   On RN ships, carronades, which came in a large variety of sizes, were nicknamed 'smashers', because of their primary function

Starboard   The right hand side of a vessel, when facing forwards.

Stays   The standing rigging set fore and aft of a mast to give longitudinal support. Sails often being set from stays on the fore side of a mast

Swivel guns   Normally small anti-personnel weapons, mounted on a swivel on the bulwarks or rails, loaded with small bags of rough shot, nails, etc. (see also Traverse guns)

Tack   A hook or tackle, attached to the lowest point of the luff of a sail leading edge, to keep it taught and make it stand to its work

Tacking   Working a ship under sails towards the wind, first tacking to one side, then back towards the other. Or the act of turning the ship through the eye of the wind from one tack to the other

Timbers   The large sectioned sawn timber forming the framework, or ribs of a vessel

Tonnage   A variety of measurements used down through the ages to indicate a vessel's size. Herein tons burthen is mainly used. That is, the notional cargo carrying capacity of a vessel expressed as a number of wine tuns. This measurement was used in calculating all sorts of dues chargeable against shipping – harbour; pilotage; light; keelage;

Train oil   Fish oil, mainly expressed from pilchards during the curing process, used to fuel pungent, smoky lamps. Possibly derived from 'strained' oil. Or from the fact that it was 'drained' along channels to collecting barrels

Traverse guns   Relatively large cannon mounted on a traverse slide amidships. This enabled it to cover a wide arc of fire, on either side, as opposed to the restricted arc on one side covered by normal broadside guns. This weapon was particularly favoured by some privateers

Victualling   Pronounced 'Vitt'ling'. The formal supply of food and drink for the consumption of the crew. In the merchant service, usually restricted to while the crew were on articles

Watches (a)   The division of the crew which, under normal conditions, allowed some hands to rest while others worked the ship. Two watches were normal on the packets, working four hours on and four hours off. The duty watch worked the sails, kept lookout, and steered the vessel. However, it was not all rest for the off duty watch, who were employed on routine maintenance tasks about the ship during daylight hours

Watches (b)   The division of the 24 hour day into a combination of four and two hour periods. Obscurely the watch cycle started with the 'First watch', 20:00 to 24:00, 'Middle watch', 00:00 to 04:00, 'Morning watch', 04:00 to 08:00, 'Forenoon watch', 08:00 to 12:00, 'Afternoon watch', 12:00 to 16:00, 'First dog-watch', 16:00 to 18:00, 'Second dog-watch', 18:00 to 20:00. Dog-watches were introduced to create an uneven number of watch periods, alternating the watch cycle every day

Weather cloths   Canvas screens secured to the open rails, acting as spray deflectors

Weather Guage   Where one vessel approaching another, is closer to the wind, that vessel is said to be holding the 'weather guage'. This position was supposed to enable a commander to press home an attack, or make his escape, more effectively

Wind & water (between)   That part of the hull alternately immersed or exposed by the waves as a ship rolls and heels to the wind

Windward   In a direction toward the wind. 'To windward' – being up wind of another vessel

Windward side   The side of the vessel facing the wind, riding high out of the water

General Index

139

Index of People

Porteous, James 111
Richards, John (1) 100
Richards, John (2) 57
Roberts, William 45
Rogers, William 6, 49–51, 104
Rogers, Zachary 36 see Packet Agents
Servante, John 46–8
Sherburn, Joseph 38, 39
Sisson, Samuel Lt. RN 132
Smale (Smail/Smaile), James Lt. RN 120, 122
St. Aubyn, John 68
Steele, Samuel (Acting) 101
Symons, William H Lt. RN 112–13
Tilly, John 56
Todd, Anthony(1) 38
Todd, Anthony (2) 39, 95
Todd, Lovell 39, 102
Uring, Nathaniel 52, 70
Vivian, John 80
Watkins, John 49, 67
Wauchope, George 74
Webbe, Charles, Lt. RN 110, 133
White, John Lt. Rn 132
Williams 39
Yescombe, Edward *42, 43*, 75, 90

General

Andrews, (Lt. Adjutant 60th Reg) 83
Arbuthnot, Carolina Emma (packet passenger) 92
Arbuthnot, Charles – Consul General at Lisbon (packet passenger) 92
Aubin, Philip 74
Austin, John (Steward) 78
Ball, Mr. (Asst. Surgeon) 68
Bassett, Sir Francis, Bart (see De Dunstanville) 44
Beck, John, Cdr RN Retired 45, 83
Bell, Henrietta 22
Bennett, John Burnett (Inspector of Packets) 18–19
Blackwell, William (packet mutineer) 106
Bogle, Robert (packet passenger) 88
Brown, James (Master RN) 118
Campbell, Colin (packet passenger) 88
Cane, Joseph (packet mutineer) 106
Clemence, Robert (seaman) 59
Clemow (Steward's Mate) 68
Clift (Customs Tidesman) 104–5
Coblin, Mr. (packet passenger) 68
Conaway, Capt Trinity House 29
Cotton, Sir Robert (PMG 1691-1708) 13
Crease (Master) 49
Cruft, Capt Trinity House 29
De Dunstanville (Bassett) Baron de 44
De Gomes (alien) *93*
Doble, Stephen (Bailiff, Trefusis) 44
Drown, William L 28
Dummer, Edmund/Edward 20, 29 *et seq*, 36–7, 57, 70, 99

Dunbar, James Capt RN 102
Dunstervill, T (Shipbuilder) 47–8
Eastman, John (ex-Master RN) 118
Elliot, James 59
Enys, Lt. John (packet passenger) 89
Etheridge, Thomas, Cdr. RN 121
Fowler, Mrs. (packet passenger) 122
Franklin, Benjamin (packet passenger) 72
Freeling, Francis (PO Sec. 1798–1836) 18, 19, 24, 35, 40, 59, 97, 106
Garnett, Randall & Brent (shipbuilders) 41
Gay, William 26 see Packet Agents
Gay, William Jnr 28
Gilbert, John (seaman) 59
Goffe, William (chronometer maker) 26
Gottlieb, (patent log inventor/manufacturer) 41
Grafton, Duke of (pension) 60
Graham, William (packet passenger) 92
Gray, Mr. (Storekeeper) 26
Handes (packet office clerk) 26, *27*
Harrington, Earl of (packet passenger) 89
Harris (Master) 39
Harris, John (Storekeeper 1819-23) 26
Henry, Ensign (packet passenger) 90
Hensen, Robert (packet passenger) 88
Howe, Lord 48
Humble, Thompson & Co. (bullion consignees) 96
Kelly, Samuel (boy/seaman) 56, 62, 63, 89
Kennedy, Capt RN 72
Killigrew, Sir Peter 9, 12
King, William, Capt RN (Admiralty Superintendent of Packets) 27, 109–10, 115, 132
Kingston, John (Navy Board Mechanist– Deptford Dock Yard) 115
Le Febre, Mr. (packet passenger) 122
Levi (packet passenger) 89
Like, Mr. J (packet passenger) 68
Lott, Charles James (packet office clerk) 26, 27
Lott, Mr. (Surveyor for the South West District) 26
Lovell, Frances 22
Lyon, Mr. John (packet passenger) 92
Manuel, Mr. (packet passenger) 122
Marlborough, Duke of (pension) 60
Marshall, Phoebe (2nd wife of John Bull) 43, 46
McKinnon, John (packetman) 59
Meek (Sailmaker) 68
Melhuish, 68
Melville, Lord (First Lord of the Admiralty) 109–10
Mitchell, Bryan (Mate) 78
Nicholls, (Surgeon) 67
Parker, John (packet mutineers' spokesman) 106
Pascoe, John (Boatswain) 78–9
Pascoe, Richard (packet mutineers' spokesman) 106
Pattison, William Moncrieff (packet passenger) 92
Pellew, Samuel (Collector of Customs, Falmouth) 67, 105
Peters, Susannah 43
Phillott, Cdr RN 83

Ship Index

Fortune 71
L'Adelaide 47
L'Insurgent 35
La Confiance 48
Le Jeune Richard (La Genie/Genii/Jenna) 5, 6, 50, 75
Reprisaille 75

Privateers – American
General Tompkin 86
Globe 49
Lee 72
Reprisal 72
Saratoga 80

Prize Vessels
Crown & Wine Cask 70
La Nostre Dame La Aimanaide 69
Margaret of Nantes 70
Mary 74
St Francis Dearis 70
St John Bonadventure 69
St John, of Bordeaux 69
St Joseph 69
Thorn 74

Naval Vessels – British
Acteon, HM Sloop 82
Britannia, HM Cutter 104
Columbine, HMS 94
Coureageux, HMS 55
Dart, HM Cutter 104
Experiment, HM Cutter (Receiving-ship) 103–4
Gannet, HMS 94
Gleaner, HM Ketch 104
Hampshire, HMS 39
Harlequin, HM Brig 83
Hawke, HMS 106
Juno, HMS 46
Lizard, HMS 39
Lurcher, HM Cutter 47
Mullet, HM Schooner 104
Niemen, HMS 106
Nimrod, HM Cutter 47
North Star, HMS 106
Plover, HM Sloop 82
Porcupine, HM Frigate 22
Poulette, HMS 102, 103
Primrose, HM Brig 59, 83
Psyche, HMS 82
Royal Oak, HMS 55
Stately, HMS 107
Virago, HMSt.V 122

Naval Vessels – French
Duc de Hanovre (L'Hanovre), Advice boat 39

L'Etoile, National frigate 80
L'Insurgente, Frigate 49
La Friponne, Frigate 40
Le Resolu, Frigate 40
La Sultane, National frigate 80
Sans Pareil 50

Other Vessels
Betsey 55
Brunswick PS 17
Congress 132
Don Juan PS 119
Royal George PS 119
Sir Francis Drake PS 17
Severn PS 120
Tay PS 122